# Escape from Teaching

# Escape from Teaching

Rolf Arnold

ROWMAN & LITTLEFIELD
Lanham • Boulder • New York • London

Published by Rowman & Littlefield
A wholly owned subsidiary of The Rowman & Littlefield Publishing Group, Inc.
4501 Forbes Boulevard, Suite 200, Lanham, Maryland 20706
www.rowman.com

6 Tinworth Street, London SE11 5AL, United Kingdom

Copyright © 2019 by Rolf Arnold
Original German manuscript translated by Glenn M. Peach

British Library Cataloguing in Publication Information Available

**Library of Congress Cataloging-in-Publication Data**

ISBN 978-1-4758-4730-7 (pbk. : alk. paper)
ISBN 978-1-4758-4731-4 (electronic)

∞™ The paper used in this publication meets the minimum requirements of American National Standard for Information Sciences—Permanence of Paper for Printed Library Materials, ANSI/NISO Z39.48–1992.

Printed in the United States of America

# Contents

# Introduction: The Reason—the Competence Catastrophe

This text is a call to action. The title *Escape from Teaching* may sound a bit like an imperative. It may even remind the reader of the short book *Time for Outrage* by the former French resistance fighter Stéphane Hessel (2011), which is cited as an inspiration for the Occupy Wall Street movement. However, the only similarities here will be found in the spirit, not the subject matter! And, considering the many long-standing traditions, viewpoints, and routines that characterize the teaching practice at most educational institutions, you should be crying out with impatience and indignation.

In many respects, education is still subject to administrative rules that discourage voicing concerns about the sustainability of skills development; many of the recent findings from educational and brain research and the potential benefits of informal and self-structured learning are never heard. Then there are the change skeptics, who seem to abound with arguments that are seldom more than a polemic or a fundamentalist position. Besides warnings ungrounded in theory that claim discipline is a necessary and feasible aspect, the reader interested in educational policy frequently encounters prophesies of doom in which the talk is of the coming "dusk and darkness" (cf. Liessmann 2016).

Such prophets want to evoke fears of dark times ahead and think they know the exact parties responsible for the decay. They identify them from their courageous efforts to transform our society's learning environment and their attempts to focus on professional forms of support for identity and skills development. In effect, by opposing such attempts, skeptics risk losing exactly what they thought was secure: *the successful education of the next generation and the current adult population.*

The actual effects of the time spent in educational institutions barely enter into the conversation: "It's fine the way it is!"—say the conservatives, where their cynicism is barely hidden from an interested public. It is time to ask

- What did we really learn from all those years that we spent in instructional and often insulting contexts?
- What have we got to show from this wealth, and what can we become as a result of this experience?
- What do we forget in such contexts, and did that deprive us of our self-confidence and self-structuring skills?
- What consequences associated with seeking and testing can equip us with permanent skills and abilities?
- How could educational institutions change to become places for successful self-directed skills development?
- How can we, as individuals and as a society, develop *the potential* that rests within us all?

The call to "escape from teaching" strengthens the thesis that something must fundamentally change in our educational institutions in terms of encounters and guidance if the individual potential to shape what we learn and the potential for self-directing lifelong learning goals are to be unlocked. Discipline and instruction as the, more or less, hidden context to which we hold ourselves and the next generation cannot continue.

The contradictions between the expectations of society and the job markets for self-structuring and the scandalous forgetfulness-effect are all too obvious. We even seem to have become accustomed to this in many areas. The social selectivity of the education system goes without mention. This book does not show us which people have failed in our educational system; rather it tells us which people our educational system has failed, day in and day out—with subtle mechanisms and often with a cynical reversal of the blame.

*Escape from Teaching* does not propose a separate educational program. It does not propose any new grammar schools—one standard for all—because, in the past, such structural recommendations were unable to achieve consensus in a society that seems more concerned with eligibility than with real learning. Equal opportunity in the various pathways to education could be increased, for example, by means of recognizing skills acquired on the job.

However, the possible impact of such structural reforms in and of themselves is generally overestimated since they do not automatically equate to greater effectiveness in learning. This text advocates rather for an internal *didactic* organizational development of educational institutions. Much evidence today shows that the learning culture and the support for long-term self-development (cf. Arnold 2013b, 2016) are the starting points for the changes needed to create a competent global community.

This is an urgent necessity. By no means are competencies currently constituted to everyone's satisfaction, as John Erpenbeck and Werner Sauter state in their book *Stop the Competence Catastrophe! Pathways to a New Education System:*[1]

> Germany is well on its way to a competence catastrophe. Its educational future is in jeopardy because it is completely ignoring the transformation to a competence society. It supports an educational system that is only able to change at a snail's pace, while the world all around is changing at a rapid tempo. In all areas of education from schools to universities to commercial enterprises, the reliance on scandalously ineffective methods of seminar learning continues, often in the form of platform instruction. Most learning still takes place in closed classrooms, lecture halls, or seminar hotels, rather than at the places where the actual challenges are to be met. Learning ought to last for a lifetime, but the world of tomorrow seldom plays a part.
>
> Knowledge transfer is considered as the ultimate wisdom, examined according to the principles of "Bulimia learning": Consume knowledge, regurgitate it for the examination—and immediately forget it. . . . Competence—the ability to self-direct and creatively manage challenges—is only mentioned in the Sunday sermons by those most responsible for education. The rather sensible approach of the Bologna Reforms is completely reversed. Successful competence development assumes the primacy of self-responsible and self-structured learning in challenging situations as well as using and preserving the competencies throughout life. The present educational systems in schools, universities, and companies ignore these requirements and hinder the necessary development of the competence society. (Erpenbeck/Sauter 2016, pp. 1–2)

The competence catastrophe is the reason for writing this book. This book does not add further to the critical review. It does not question or criticize the efforts of so many teachers and trainers in schools and businesses. Rather, the objective is to set the stage for internal discussions at educational institutions and to identify the starting points for the urgently needed changes in our learning culture. The text may encourage educators, in school, vocational training, university, and adult education programs, to reflect critically on their own teaching-learning practices.

## NOTE

1.  cf. colearnall.wordpress.com (visited February 5, 2017).

*Chapter 1*

# The Human Species Is Capable of Learning

It is truly astonishing that human beings—an animal that comes into this world so weak, in need of care and protection for years before gaining the strength to care for itself, an evolutionary weakling—clearly won the battle of the species to capture and dominate the top rung of the food chain. When seeking an explanation for this success we stumble, in particular, over what the anthropologists and experts in human history point out as the only reason for this outcome: *the human ability to learn.*

The nearly infinite ability to learn from experience, to try out new and better solutions to problems, and to successfully adapt to the surroundings can already be observed in small children. Incredible as it is, we observe the ease with which they learn to talk—and, if necessary, even master several languages simultaneously.

They learn independently how to walk and acquire increasing complex abilities to orient in a social setting. Surely, they are imitating models and following examples, but more than that, people do not only adopt what is handed down, but also vary, experiment, and innovate to create new forms of expression. We are made to live in a world of seemingly never-ending learning processes, where a cognitive-emotional *transformation* takes place, for which we do not yet have the concepts needed to fully understand.

For the purposes of this book, the fine difference in the verbs to "adapt" versus to "adopt" can be misleading, so although still not exact, the term to "appropriate" is most useful. From everything we know today, learning is an action on the part of the learner, who can be stimulated and guided, but not really forced. People learn, just as they breathe—in regular spurts, never stopping, sometimes flat, sometimes deep down, occasionally halting, but not for long.

You cannot *not* learn, just as you cannot *not* breathe. Just as no one in a breathing class ever teaches us to take a breath, we do not have to learn how to actively appropriate something from our surroundings. Although *resuscitation* may occasionally be required in extreme situations, it is only a temporary measure to help when the breathing function of the lungs is impaired. Learning is different: although we are taught, we can learn (only) on our own. The consequences are serious: the inherent learning function of our brains can switch to stand-by, and we can become increasingly helpless learners.

The term *to appropriate* helps us better understand the intransitive effect of these interrelationships on learning. The adjective "intransitive," although borrowed from grammar theory, is chosen deliberately. Originally, "intransitive" was used to describe action verbs that do not need an object to receive the action. The verb "to learn" must also manage without an object since no child can learn until the cognitive processes create something and allow self-development to occur.

This was already noted by Jean Piaget (1896–1980), who pointed out that in childhood learning, it is the child who independently produces the content *from the depth of the soul*. This intransitive logic does not merely apply to childhood learning, but it also figures in the lifelong learning of adolescents and adults.

## IN FOCUS: THE "REFLEXIBLE MAN"

The European education debate began in the 1990s with efforts to propose a new understanding of learning. It featured a shift to the self. Educators began to have a clearer focus on the fact that it is life experience that supports (or hinders) the formation of an individual to his or her full inner potential. The criticism of the current forms of education and training of the younger generation also underwent a fresh new revival.

In particular, the learning culture at educational institutions (at schools and universities) was critically reviewed, revealing unintended and often paralyzing side effects that increasingly lead to a sheer irreconcilable contrast to what is required for a future-oriented set of competencies. At the same time, there was a return to the informal and self-directed appropriation and maturation processes, in which people can develop their own potential.

However, this turning toward the self was only sporadically joined by an aversion to the forms of institutionalized education, as was typical with the pedagogic reform at the turn of the century or the anti-pedagogy of the 1970s. The impulse often resulted in an anti-establishment attitude and generally disappeared without effect.

Since the 1990s, the "new pedagogic reform" has focused on the issue of how educational organizations like schools, universities, and training centers—with their self-image and their mission and range of services—can redefine themselves as places for sustainable acquisition of essential future competencies; and it has asked what transformation processes are required.

The aim of these efforts was also new. Rather than swearing to some notions of self-fulfillment, the efforts were a rather pragmatic examination of the competencies that enable a person to shape an otherwise uncertain future. Over time, not only the real competence-destroying effect of highly selective education practices came under suspicion, but the tasks themselves were seen as doing more harm than good. The rapidly spreading movement to promote the development of the "flexible man"[1] (cf. Sennett 1998) was met with some skepticism: clearly hidden behind this movement were the old linear-mechanistic hopes.

The linear-mechanistic assumption employed in some forms of educational practices that it is not only possible—but also acceptable—to "produce" the type of person capable and willing to adapt to the changing demands in the labor market and the society overall! These hopes harbored no illusions that such a person would ever access: "what being human really means" (or could mean). Advocates of the use of the linear-mechanistic concept were willing to accept—once again—the production of universally employable individuals who would later be unable to use the learning in the interests of reason, humanity, and solidarity.

Fortunately, such restricted functionalist concepts mostly disappear without effect because of a growing social awareness by the public regarding a values orientation in addition to a renewed focus on public responsibility in educational matters. Specifically, the responsible public is obligated to design education programs that consider the expectations of the individual and society—not just a particular group. The principles of fairness and equal opportunity are just as essential in measuring the success of education as is the creation of professional and personal opportunities for shaping experiences and the future.

Unlike the natural sciences, which are bound to the ideal of objectivity, education theorists and teachers are normatively tied to observe, interpret, understand, and suggest. A review and evaluation of education must consider not only conformity with the requirements of the job market and society but also the provisos of support and guidance for individualization. The responsible actors must not only follow the idol of the "flexible man", but also the "reflexive man"—thus: the "reflexible man.[2]

Educators are aware of the self-absorbing power of habits and strong attachments to their own traditions and experiences, knowing that these are what always tempt them to hold to their beliefs and to construct a future on the basis of past experiences. They are aware that this helps in making the future look, more or less, like the past has already looked.

The "reflexible man" demonstrates not only flexibility, but such a person also tries to reflect. For such persons, they know that they can change their world only if they succeed in changing themselves. As they learn to judge a situation less quickly, they open up to strangers, the unknown, and perhaps, some previously rejected options. They appreciate comparisons where, previously, snap judgments sufficed to create clarity.

At least now, the prerequisites are satisfied to reveal a different reality—a different perspective of reality. The reflexible man does not merely adapt to supposed or actual givens but possesses a unique flexibility owing to a self-tuning skill. In this context, self-tuning is an expression of the ability to learn, an inner potential.

The reflexible man also seeks knowledge in order to be able to examine, judge, and act. Yet the nature of this knowledge is different. It represents an integration of factual relationships with our own abilities, and it is used in the development of our own opinions or to initiate a constructive effort to find a solution. Developing this ability to manage and use knowledge demands other guidance than simple lesson plans or modular manuals.

What is truly required is the methodical strengthening of the student's social, emotional, and reflective faculties—in coming to terms with the issues of content. The reflexible man not only learn "something," but expand on their own individual abilities

- to develop sources of knowledge,
- to deal with the new,
- to plan and design self-learning projects, and
- to change their familiar views and routines.

Over time, the learning individual becomes more and more that person they have always been—sometimes without realizing it, taking ownership of the learning—a process of reappropriation that is not to be underestimated in a democratic society, a job market, or in shaping the lifelong learning society.

In the process, knowledge changes from a mere possession to a complex ability to change your thinking and actions from an individual basis to consider the qualities shared in common with others. Norbert Ricken and Uwe Schimank remind us of what can be viewed as "good" in their introduction at the 24th Bremen University Discourses, when they spoke of a common conviction in Greek philosophy and the European enlightenment:

> Good is when knowledge replaces ignorance and when scientifically verified knowledge replaces mere experience, and that individual and social progress is advancing precisely in this direction. (Ricken/Schimank 2012, p.11)

This orientation is not questioned in the restitution of learning. No one doubts the importance of moving from ignorance or superficial knowledge to having real knowledge, or even the importance of expertise for taking appropriate action. The aim is not to have the learners assume enlightened beliefs or expertise, but rather to make these accessible to learners who are able to develop it themselves. The central issue for the reflexible man is to seek the path of self-discovery. A parallel question is what the role of the teacher is, or could be, in this self-formation.

The task ultimately faces the basic paradox of all pedagogy, how to lead people to freedom—a movement whose patronizing substance, in essence, seems to reject the aim itself. Despite this contradictory nature, in the end, this effect must occur for the competencies required for autonomous problem solving to work. Essentially, autonomy cannot be practiced pro forma or in some weakened form—as something like "light" autonomy. When people really learn to express themselves and have the chance to practice and connect with their expected abilities, they retain an indelible potential.

---

### TEXTBOX 1.1

In this sense, autonomy is experienced internally as something irreversible, always pushing to be expressed anew even if, initially, the workplace environment does not seem to allow it or, perhaps, even impedes it.

On closer examination, the reflexible man's abilities constitute what the main theories of education have said all along: to provide the preparation needed to strengthen a person left to his or her own devices.

---

The question of how to achieve such strength is answered differently in the competence theories than in the education theories. They expect less from the input, asking instead for successful self-reinforcement and behavioral outcomes that show whether something was skillful or not. Competence models are less reliant on curricula, preferring to follow the psychologically established view of the concepts of *self-realization* and *self-assertion*.

The fundamental idea is that competencies are identity elements that both enrich and expand the individual's self-expression and behavioral disposition. Therefore, the learner-identity connection to the competence theories is evidently more important than the connection to content and requirement catalogs. These fade to the background to give greater focus to the content of the competencies themselves. Success in education takes on a whole new meaning: it can hardly be defined as curricular any longer, but it can be specified more or less with a precise and binding description of required abilities or competencies.

Any analysis of the possible educational effect of teaching and subject matter must proceed from a different perspective, or must even be replaced by an "analysis of the learner." The learning movement expected to come from the person must first be backed by the person and arranged as a subjectively relevant learning movement.

The desired competence does not become permanent simply because a didactic analysis of content presents the present, future, and other relevancies and anchors them in the curriculum. Even the competence-building effect of the content can only develop when placed within the horizon of the search radar of the learner. This enabling turn away from teaching content toward an analysis of the learner assumes:

> Appropriation movements do not [follow] a technical but rather a subjective logic—this is clearly a collectivization of the predominantly formal didactic approach! The learning success is not produced by professional structures, but from the respective horizons of the learner's biographic and environmental precedents. . . .
>
> Modern didactics calls for process competency that allows the other person to talk, "to link" effectively with the professional topics and required competencies and to effectively support the individual learner's professional and extracurricular searching movements. The success of such a "learning guide" requires a three-fold expansion of the view, so often narrowed by formal didactics. This didactic assumes the educational "power of content" is limited and does not, per se, enable development: What is more important for the sustained maturation of competency is the participation and self-empowerment of the learner, because even professional competencies developed from one single understanding can become rigid in the solutions experienced in a lifetime. (Arnold 2013a, p. 221)

This "extension of professional teaching" (ibid., p. 222) is accompanied by a fundamental shift of the didactic reasoning and thematic structure of teaching-learning programs. It sharpens the focus on the actual benefits of staging opportunities for appropriation and competence development, as shown in the comparison in table 1.1.

## SAYING GOODBYE TO THE DELUSION OF OMNISCIENCE

The idea of complete knowledge can never be the point of learner-focused teaching. Of course, certified graduates should have the basic competence to access the expert knowledge necessary to act, intervene, and shape their domain.

**Table 1.1. From content to learner didactic (see Klafki 1993; Arnold 2016, p. 181*ff.*)**

| *Didactic analysis of the content→* | | *Didactic analysis of the learner* | |
|---|---|---|---|
| **Justification** | | | |
| Present importance | What is the present goal and the topic relationship to the learner's everyday world? | Learning project-reference | Is the learner already trapped in his or her own attempted explanation/clarification? |
| Future importance | What significance will the topic have for the learner in the future? | Self-learning reference | How does the learner learn and what preparations are taken for the—unknown—future? |
| Sample importance | What general relationships, connections, regulations, etc., can be worked out with the help of this topic? | Individualize | How are the learner's values appreciated and supported to help—under his or her terms—the learner's search? |
| **Thematic structuring** | | **Situation** | |
| Structure of the content | What thematic structure does the topic have? Under what perspective does the work take place? What is the methodical structure of the topic? What is the larger context of the topic? What is required of the learner? | Situational orientation | How can you account for the fact that people prefer to develop lasting skills in stable situations? |
| Testability and verifiability | What abilities, insights, and forms of action must be present for the learning process to be successful? | Skills development | How can learners self-assess their progress and the state of their abilities? |
| **Accessibility** | | **Utility** | |
| Access and presentation options | How can the topic be presented and made accessible? | Access paths | How can various learning paths be opened simultaneously without having to wander through in lockstep? |

*(Continued)*

**Table 1.1.  (Continued)**

| *Didactic analysis of the content→* | | *Didactic analysis of the learner* | |
| --- | --- | --- | --- |
| **Methodical structure** | | **Staging** | |
| Choice of method | What methodical structure is suitable for the topic? How can active learning and an active debate process with the aim of codetermination and solidarity be promoted through method selection? | Arrangement | How can classrooms be designed to allow the learners to use their own self-directed learning methods? |

However, they do not need all of the knowledge all of the time, and generally, graduates retain a deeper competence in *those* areas in which they could already practice them, while other—necessary—knowledge fades and falls into the background. We master it for an examination, but not for practice. In place of the binding horizons of interpretation, forms of argument, traditional beliefs, or an ethical-moral framework, the varying layers of solitude, discontinuity, and uncertainty are met only by the "force" of the learner, which may merely have a formal description.

The English word *reflexible* in this book is an adjective to describe what is really at the core of this competence-focused approach: The "reflexible man" introduced on the preceding pages is not merely a "flexible man" (Sennett 1998). Subjectivity requires, ultimately, to simultaneously balance many contrasts and to express them appropriately in each situation; to deal with external demands as well as increase your own inner strengths, to preserve continuity and have the courage to innovate, and to keep a professional distance from the enclosure forming around you.

To survive in a rapidly changing world, the reflexible man must break free from the delusion of complete knowledge. Klafki's didactic analysis is not in the interest of a completeness of content requirement, but rather a representative nature, that is, a reasonable selection of content from the great abundance of possible knowledge. This intentional incompleteness is designed to emphasize the learner. It avoids the debate over, for example, what students should learn and, instead, is more concerned with clarifying the way experiences are stored and how autonomy can be cultivated.

Additionally, it subordinates everything else while clinging to the outstanding developmental tasks of the learner. By enabling autonomous learning and assuming the ability to gain access to the required topics, to go into more depth, and to practice possible applications, the analysis anticipated what would ultimately be confirmed in the serious debate over competence theory.

Namely, the claim of omniscience is an expression of an obsolete understanding of teaching: it neglects the desperate search for self-structured forms of learning and shaping the advanced areas of our society and how it will most surely be expressed in the context of digitalization and the workplace of tomorrow (cf. Kucklick 2015).

The Vodafone Foundation's "Search for the Appropriate Education for the Digital Age" (Vodafone 2016) also calls for activation over completeness. Among others, Stephen Spurr argues for the "converted classroom" designed to reinforce individualized learning and provide a "path to a liberalized world of independent research possibilities" (Spurr 2016, p. 47):

> The valuable time when present in the classroom can be put to better use—and not wasted through repetition, or the copying of notes from a PowerPoint presentation or from a long-winded lecture. Students are prepared for each classroom hour and are immediately involved in discussions or written individual or group exams that are intended to promote learning. Teachers must really start to think seriously about how to enable this deeper kind of learning. It demands excellent planning. The instructional tempo is not the main consideration. It is rather about the tempo and quality of the learning itself and developing analytical creative thinking skills. (ibid.)

In this concept of digital education, the completeness or representativeness of the content takes a distant second place to the individual development of the ability to appropriate and to structure knowledge. It is about enabling a broad universe of thinking, not supporting the tendency to measure and regiment.

## NOTES

1. The flexible man, but in the sense of "human being" that does not express sex or gender (in German – *Der flexible Mensch*).
2. "Reflexible", in this context, refers to a portmanteau of the words reflexive and flexible.

*Chapter 2*

# We Can Learn, but We Cannot Be Taught

The more we view learning as a lifetime movement, the more teaching fades into the background (cf. Siebert 2015). Although learners are curious about their environment and accumulate experience, they often follow provisos, instructions, and doctrine only to avoid detriments or disadvantages. Certainly, some people can achieve remarkable things in this way: eventually, they can actually show what is expected of them. They are even able to memorize lessons and reproduce them.

However, these newly acquired abilities are usually quickly lost as soon as the pressure of expectation diminishes and no occasion is found to integrate the acquired content into their own experience and to construct a learning movement of their own. Only in the luckiest cases do learners grasp what is forced on them and then it is because they have established access—their access—to process the new perspectives, even though the whole staging had nothing at all to do with their questions and their learning movements.

The broad drain of knowledge is an expression of the fact that much content and even entire subjects in school curricula are irrelevant: they are mastered under pressure for as long as the expectation of social survival lasts, only to fade away in real life. How many school years are reduced in this way after a reasonable period of consideration to a laughably low proficiency? Many are the times we look back and think about what we once knew and once could do.

We accept the wasted time as a necessary part of our fate—not suspecting that we were also losing touch with our own learning ability. "We are learning for school, not for life!" is the motto of this institutionalized kind of learning. This presents itself to us in an ambivalent way: On one hand, the institutionalization of learning opened up broad social access to education and, in retrospect, is seen as a necessary element of the true democratization of the various forms of human cooperation.

On the other hand, this advantage has been purchased by the devaluation of informal forms of learning and personality development, whereby the fundamental relevancy of this has come under public scrutiny only since the end of the last century (cf. Rohs 2016). The "recognition of prior learning," as demanded by the EU education policy, is a determined effort to acknowledge the fact that not only schools educate, but so does life, as Pestalozzi proposed (cf. Bittner 2011).

A rudimentary approach is now starting to take shape in the didactic itself (i.e., the manner in which the teaching process is organized and staged), as this turns toward an acceptance of informal learning. Yet knowledge-oriented teaching is still dominant and primacy continues to be assigned to content and instruction, unaffected by the doubts put forth in recent years by brain and cognition researchers about the likelihood of mediating content. Only a scattered few radically question this approach and call, for example, for the "end of didactics."

The mainstream continues to follow the path of irrelevant education: learners are "shown," relationships are "explained," and standards are "dictated" as their relevance to competence development is questionable. Ultimately, this expository method is defended with the comment that standards are not open for discussion, which is why it is necessary to present and justify them and to demand they be followed as if any questioning of the teaching of standards is actually questioning the standards themselves.

To be perfectly clear: of course, human civilization is supported by shared worldviews and compliance with achieved standards in task organization. However, these must be appropriated, modified, and personalized by the learners in order to deliver on their promises as we expect over the long term.

In this context, the "hidden agenda" of this kind of instruction must not be overlooked. The real question to be asked is: What do people permanently learn, if they learn to adapt but not to appropriate? The most important lesson in all this, of course, is that knowledge and abilities having been once acquired are then lost! Students must submit to learning requirements that have nothing to do with them and their self-learning movements and do not lead to permanent results.

It is not what we can do or what we know that determines our chances in life, but rather what we have once known and done—the quintessential learning from experience so to speak! People learn to accept the loss as an unavoidable side effect of learning. Not infrequently they even lose faith in the fact that their own learning is what can provide them with the permanent subjective faculties that enable them to shape their lives differently, in previously unknown variety and depth. This loss of confidence in our own learning powers is what weakens, if not breaks, people as many examples of "black pedagogy" now show.

While the effect may be exactly what the authorities (government, churches, and the wealthy) in authoritarian societies have evidently set as a goal, it often proves to be a hindrance, if not even counterproductive, in modern, dynamic, evolving societies. As they march into an unknown future, such societies increasingly require people who have developed confidence in their own powers of learning and are capable of engaging in self-organized social activities. Perhaps for the first time in history, we find ourselves today in the midst of a social change in which economic and social needs coincide with the requirement for a program of broad learner development.

Precisely because the future is unknown, we need more than the handed down methods. We need suitable problem-solving skills, which must be developed and shaped—often "at eye level." These solutions demand personal, professional, and social competence from the actors, who can successfully develop these skills only from within and not in the context of adaptation, instruction, or even discipline.

It is time to accept the conclusions unanimously reached and recommended by cognitive and brain research. We must finally admit that while people are able to learn, they cannot be taught. This requires a deeper insight into what learning actually is, in order to gradually leave behind those traditional forms of institutionalized teaching/learning processes that express instructional logic—which has little to recommend itself other than the force of habit, that is, bad habits.

## THE THREE LEVELS OF DIDACTIC THEORY

Already clear in the introduction is the fact that this new view of learning and the appropriation of knowledge follows a learner-oriented perspective (refer to figure 2.1). Even expert or technical requirements for problem solving are more focused now than in the past on understanding the learner's search or appropriation movements.

The requirements are not all that different or independent from the learner, or as constructivists say—the observer. They are created in the consciousness of each learner in his or her own special way, that is, against the background of his or her own experiences and habits (routine approaches, paradigms, etc.). This is a subjective-emergent act, which is supported and accompanied by external stimuli but is not effectively shaped by them.

The didactic-methods question "How should learners learn?" meets the curricular question "What should learners learn?" (Arnold/Gómez Tutor 2007, p. 40). The result is a specification of tasks for a new definition of the relationship between knowledge and learning.

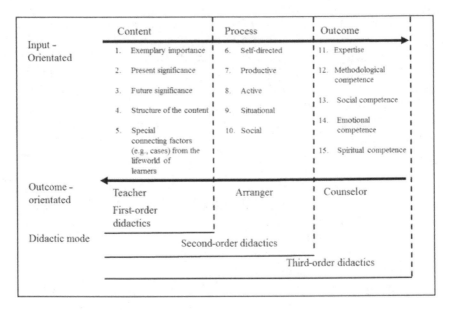

**Figure 2.1.   From first-order to third-order didactics**

The overview in figure 2.1 summarizes the didactic debate over the criteria required for successful education. It lays out a path for shaping the ever-changing meaning of expertise and is directed more at the integration and less at the replacement of the previous, mainly content-oriented teaching models. For the didactic of the "third order," content and process dimensions are accorded a greater focus in an outcome- or competence-oriented model. Representativeness, structural relevance, and content completeness are not the only criteria deemed essential for a successful education.

Rather, the expanded view of competence takes in dimensions that describe a person's identity and competence development on the level of the learner and finds expression in the methodical and social as well as in the emotional and spiritual forms of dealing with reality. This last dimension, in particular, is gladly overlooked in the discourse and is subject to an esoteric suspicion—a reluctance that misses the basic importance of a person's own values in the autonomous shaping of his or her own life as well as for dealing with life's changing situations.

Frequent discussions about the importance of attitude are fine, but they avoid a central element of successful education by failing to specify the inner abilities needed to form value-based attitudes. Astin and others are right when they speak of a "potentially very important topic" and complain: "The development of self-awareness receives very little attention in our colleges and universities" (Astin et al. 2011, p. 2).

In nearly all areas of our education system, the priority is on content and de facto learning. These concepts are input oriented and are only just beginning to have access to an outcome-oriented justification for competence development. This situation must fundamentally change in the face of the transformation of knowledge in postmodern societies and the increase in technological (educational) storage, retrieval, presentation, and handling (cf. Nowotny/ Scott/Gibbson 2001).

We do not want to attempt to shape the fluid topics of the future using the content-based learning concepts of the past, which would be as absurd as trying to run a global trade business from a covered wagon. Our educational institutions are still far from the ideal of a competence-building culture of self-structured learning. In their latest publication, *Stop the Competence Catastrophe*, Erpenbeck and Sauter focus sharply on the university tradition of showing and instructing:

> Good university lecturers, as responsible scientists, always know that their lectures, given to 200 to 300 students, may provide the latest breakthroughs for specialists, but only a fraction of that is retained and still much less for effective action. Lectures are generally useless because they provide knowledge in and of itself, but hardly any knowledge for us. (Erpenbeck/Sauter 2016, p. 12)

Now this may be a rather pointed assessment and, in some cases, perhaps inappropriate, but is it wrong? Are we really doing enough

- to address the learners in their lifeworld and biographical learning projects,
- to enable the inside-out process of self-education,
- to directly promote the learner's self-learning and self-management abilities, and
- to offer them suitable learning arrangements for guided self-education, much as distance learning institutions have provided e-learning or experience-based approaches for adult education for many years?

Bill Gates made the prophecy in 2010 that in five years' time "the best lectures in the world would all be available online for free" and this would be "better than any university."[1]—True?—Not yet. Still, does it automatically follow that the present state should be grandfathered? Stephan Weichert, professor for journalism at the Hamburg Media School, defends this idea in a blanket argument:

> Neither the best lectures in the world are available for free online, nor are most offers useful over the long term. Our cold universities made of exposed concrete and linoleum still exist in a world of things. Even classroom attendance has not disappeared, perhaps because the deal with the supervising professor, who is

drinking wine somewhere on the Atlantic coast, is simply too good to be true. (Weichert 2016)[2]

If it is true that knowledge and competence cannot be imparted, but can only be independently appropriated and developed by each learner—as every respected brain researcher emphatically insists in the pedagogic discourse without much resonance (Roth/Lück 2010)—then we just cannot continue to do what we are doing in our schools, colleges, and universities. The learners must urgently return back to the core of competence development, where they have been all along in their adult education.

Since the 1980s, adult teaching has pursued a line that systematically studies and theoretically describes learning *in the interpretative mode* as a *searching movement to find individual identity and competencies* and as a *transformation of common knowledge* as well as an *expansion or strengthening of the self.* However, this follows the intransitive pedagogic discourse as promoted by the vast majority of those who express an opinion on education policy and call, for example, for a show of courage, crackdowns, and consequences in the classroom, while not even beginning to understand the approach.

This comes as no surprise, for through our transitive use of language, we are compelled to understand what can only be understood with our terms and concepts:

> Let us have a closer look at the concept of education itself. The associated root is the verb "to educate" and is a transitive verb and refers to an accusative object. Verbum Transitivum means: "Verb that transcends into an object" (Kluge). An educator, a person whose activity is to educate, "transcends" to an object, or educates another person. This view corresponds to current pedagogic thinking. When speaking of youth education, adult education, and teacher training, etc. we normally mean the activities of people who engage in the education of other people (youths, adults, and student teachers). This concept of education is technically a working concept. It was first used as such in the 18th century, when the task of education was to create enlightened (as perfect as possible) people and make them (as useful as possible) citizens. (Sesink 2006, p. 17)

In contrast, the recent findings of brain research and cognitive learning studies lead instead to an *intransitive* understanding of the learning and teaching processes, which strengthens the autonomy of the learner, in other words, the principally self-organized confrontation with new requirements and competence development.

These latest theories do not follow the logic of knowledge transfer or instruction, but rather the individual's specific patterns of appropriation. It is an attempt to establish and shape competence development and a more learner-oriented approach to learning and to define a more precise concept of knowledge than what is generally suggested by *showing* or *opening* knowledge to a new generation (cf. Türcke 2016). Not everything that is is relevant for the development of future abilities in the different domains and training courses!

---

**TEXTBOX 2.1**

People can know a lot and still do nothing (cf. Arnold/Erpenbeck 2014), and human beings—an animal that learns—can learn with the passage of time not to learn anymore. When this happens, the natural curiosity is paralyzed, and the abilities to discover yourself and your world, to experiment with innovative ideas, and to grow beyond what already exists, are wasted.

---

## THE FLEETING NATURE OF KNOWLEDGE

Modern societies are often referred to as knowledge societies, but that in no way means there is a consensus about what this knowledge is and how it changes and how it has changed in content over the years. We encounter knowledge as an external supposition and an imposition—something facing us. It bundles the wealth of views and interpretations of *the* situations, which we have to deal with as human beings.

These descriptions have a history of discussion. They are checked, tested, modified, and refined or rejected—in any case, they arrive with the force of fact that is hardly open for discussion. This "safe" supply of knowledge is what we deliver and share with the next generation.

Cultures and societies differ in how they legitimize their safe knowledge base and in the ways they regulate the dispute over the validity of our perceptions and arguments. Ultimately, knowledge societies are "open societies" in the proposals of Karl Popper. They are carried by the practice of a discourse, "which admits that I might be wrong, you might be right and, perhaps, together we can come to the truth" (Popper 1957, p. 267).

The approach demands both external and inner openness. It is essentially democratic, yet it also focuses on the actor's inner openness to questioning and new clarifications. Totalitarian rules of validity and subordination are replaced with scientific thinking and the institutionalization of critique. Without the external openness guaranteed by the state, it is difficult for the inner openness to develop and to focus on the circumstances. Where habits, opinions, and basic attitudes determine what is applicable; not only scientific advances but also social and individual progress is also left behind.

The knowledge regarded as safe in a society is what creates the more or less "binding content" for its schools, universities, and vocational training facilities, in addition to the continuous education providers (Hof 2016, p. 205). This content is selected, justified, curricularized, and didactically prepared—not always while excluding the public, but—allowing for exceptions—mainly in the shadowy areas of the governmental departments, education commissions, and school boards.

The foremost goal of this social construction of content is to enable the next generation and adult students to participate in the discourse and, ultimately, to ensure the society has a general public in the first place. Both "live" from the acknowledged content and the accepted forms of exchange, as well as the justification of applicability and the implications. This concept of knowledge is social theory. It is focused on the necessities and advantages that accrue when the members of a society relate to a common inventory of interpretations, methods of handling knowledge, and argumentative styles that enable "responsible" social participation.

This description is not an exhaustive listing of the functions of knowledge. The remaining questions to be asked are: Where does knowledge come from? How does information become knowledge? And, what kind of knowledge is it?

Knowledge—at least initially—is the overall socially accepted effort to find interrelationships and to improve the effectiveness of the human endeavor.

This knowledge confronts us as explanations, not so much as detailed knowledge, but more as details embedded in structures, conceptual clarifications, regularities, and so on. "The world to be learned" (Göhlich et al. 2014, p. 7) does not encounter us as such, but rather always in the light of the contemporary, interrelated explanations. These are constantly changing and deepening as we come to understand the connections more closely over the centuries and decades and often gain the power to effectively shape them. This applies not only to the relationships in the natural sciences but also, especially, to the particular social interactions that we understand better today than fifty years ago.

Discussing knowledge in this context shows that the concept of knowledge also expresses a progression that differentiates between no knowledge and partial knowledge. This marks a sequence of steps in the development of a worldview, which leads to an increasing coherence and consistency of knowledge. These steps can be labeled "descriptive value," "explanatory value," "absence of inner conflict," "absence of external conflict," and "verifiability" (Vollmer 1991, p. 765).

## EDUCATION THROUGH EVIDENCE

The person educated by such evidence is a special kind of knowledge carrier: such people have abilities that are not exhausted in knowing the facts or in declarative knowledge (know that). Their abilities include the competence to manage and construct their own knowledge (know-how) or, as Anderson (1976) defined it, to use the procedural knowledge referred to by Christiane Hof:

> As it relates to pedagogic issues, declarative knowledge refers to learning domain related facts, while procedural knowledge refers to appropriating the ability to do certain things. This refers to certain capabilities or skills and strategies that support a person in carrying out an activity. While declarative knowledge can be called conscious and explicit, procedural know how is characterized by the fact that it is only partially convertible and has an implicit component. (Hof 2016, p. 207)

This difference leads to the question of what is actually meant when we speak of the knowledge society or the aging of knowledge. Do both kinds of knowledge age alike? Or are we simply dealing with a *knowledge shift* powered by the growing importance of procedural over declarative knowledge?

On deeper examination of the observable knowledge shift, we find that the question "On what evident knowledge can I base my thoughts and actions?" is replaced with the question "How can I be more evidence-oriented in what I think and do?" The constant concern for evidence would be an illustration of procedural knowledge. This may leave the impression of the declarative, which always seems to have the feel of something final, noticeably behind and the actors inwardly open to the new. Is that not the real task of education in a knowledge society?

Yet evidence may also be transitory. Not every evidence-based assessment can stand the test of time, as the example of Samuel Arbesman illustrates (Arbesman 2012). But people have nothing else than the mechanisms of a social construct of the evidence. Evidence-based thinking and acting logically proceeds from the experienced, not necessarily from the actual knowledge—a differentiation that is sometimes forgotten. Our justification of evidence follows social rules, for example

- interests must be excluded in the context of judgments and decisions about what applies or should apply;
- checking the validity of an assessment is always temporary, that is, it happens without any regard for the person who made the assessment; and

• recognized experts watch over which new insights derive from professional and methodical standards and which do not—a rather ambivalent "security" because it measures against the old and, perhaps, just for that reason is excluding innovation.

In particular, the natural sciences have developed forms of social control used by the scientific community to monitor the respective disciplines, who may publish what results in the respected journals and who and what may not. At the same time, these journals have various "impact factors," which as a consequence means that the chances of receiving an appointment and research resources increase only if published in a journal that has a high impact factor.

Clearly, this practice opens the door to arbitrariness, manipulation, and corruption. Authors are sometimes pressured, for example, to *carry out coercive citations* requests (by the respective journal itself just to increase their impact factor), as discovered by many recent studies (cf. Kaube 2008). A sociological critique will arrive at the rather damning conclusion that

> the peer review is not a scientific measure for the quality of the publication, but rather a social institution to calibrate the reading time for each discipline. (Hirschauer 2004, p. 62)

Meanwhile, the critiques of the actual quality of the practice of peer reviews cannot be overlooked. Interestingly, twelve articles published in the previous year and a half were resubmitted in 1982 to the same twelve professional psychology journals, and the thirty-eight referees noticed only three of them. Of the remaining nine articles, eight were rejected because of "serious methodological deficiencies"—in other words: the same articles that several months earlier had successfully passed the review process (Peters/Ceci 1982).

Such findings reinforce doubt about the quality assurance effect of this kind of publication control. It is discredited not only because of the aforementioned shameful contradictions, not to mention the arbitrariness of repeated review, but more fully by their inability to exclude exaggerations and errors in the reported research results, as John P.A. Ioannidis found in at least a third of the medical research published in peer-reviewed journals in 2005 (Ioannidis 2005).

Against the background of such inconsistencies, is it far-fetched to distrust the evidence-preserving effect of the peer review process and the so-called impact factors? And let's not forget the question of how creativity and innovativeness can be requested in the scientific disciplines when the newcomers have to submit to validity checks in the publication of their findings, where the validity of the check itself is in doubt and, furthermore, measures the new against the standards of the established mainstream.

It cannot be emphasized clearly enough: that through the rules of peer reviews, impact factors, and rankings, the record of evidence is the result of a social construct of reality. Even in this case, we can share reality only through our conditions and procedures or those of the guild, that is, in a form that affects us. What is not published is not per se unsuitable, but it is simply rarely seen and, therefore, has less impact. On the other hand, it can be assumed that studies that are accessible and gain broad acceptance, pass the reviews, and justify more meaningful action—at least temporarily—must show a more or less accurate picture—not in terms of the external reality, but as the momentarily shared basis of a functioning or socially acceptable action.

How fragile this basis is can be shown by the discussions about former U.S. Vice President Al Gore's film *An Unpleasant Truth* in 2006. In the end, even Al Gore can only present scientometric or bibliometric arguments, for example, when he soberly notes that increasingly fewer studies over the years are questioning the influence of man on global warming effect (cf. Beck 2010). The direct evidence in his own records are not adequate; he must substantiate them with indirect evidentiary records.

Climate change may be obvious, but evidence will only become fact when it is socially shared, a detail that is often overlooked and placed in opposition to constructivist epistomology theories. For example, the seemingly never-ending polemic against the systemic-constructivist view of the world is overlooked in pedagogy: Evidence is similar to truth, meaning it is—momentarily—the most reasonable conclusion, but it is still not the truth itself, as clearly shown in the history of scientific errors (Zankl 2004). To become a—temporary—truth, it must first be socially accepted.

## A BRIEF DIGRESSION: HOW STRONG IS THE EVIDENCE?

Evidence is the information that seems to explain the case. The fact that others also assess a situation as we do lets us feel secure—though not always justifiably as we know from the many paradigm changes throughout the history of science. Some scientists too easily confuse evidence with truth and abuse all those who unreasonably approach such questions more cautiously and full of doubt. Consequently, the materialists and so-called new realists respond with similar arguments. Both unanimously hold to the illusion of a safe perception of the world—how else could they assert what they assert?

The fact that these are assertions, or more precisely, stubborn assertions, is clear from the words of the philosopher Markus Gabriel, a spokesman for the new realism. When in place of an argument, he simply says: "But it is simply not true that we are always or mostly deceived" (Gabriel 2013, p. 13).

Realists or—even more extreme—materialists also wrestle with this in the pedagogic discourse. The materialistic education theories use Gamm's rehabilitation of rationalism as a kind of "radical rationalism," which holds that knowledge "unflinchingly adheres to the full autonomy of nature" and also has an obligation to the "process of emancipation of the species" (Gamm 1983, pp. 21–69).

This attitude presupposes the steadfastness of knowledge, which according to more recent theories does not exist. More specifically, it gives us the stronger impression that our own reflection allows us to think only of what is already within us as a possibility, and there is no way to really guarantee the promises consistently made by the materialistic theories, namely "the nervous system takes in information and uses it to create representations (i.e., internal images) of the surroundings" (Pongratz 2010, p. 284), while acting as if these images were somehow exact reproductions of the external world—this is reality and no other.

It goes without saying that such naive realism has won few friends even in the natural sciences, as already shown by the epistemological works in the field of physics. For example, the theoretical physicist David Bohm in his work titled *On Dialog* also dealt with the irresolvable interrelationships between the observer and the observed and stated:

> Normally, we do not realize that our assumptions influence the character of our observations. Yet, assumptions do affect the way in which we see things, how we experience things and consequently, what we want to do. In a sense, we see through our assumptions. . . . The observer is the observed. If we are unable to see the two together, the observer and the observed, i.e., the assumptions and emotions, we get a totally wrong picture. If I say I want to see what is going on in my mind, but do not think about my assumptions, I will get the wrong picture, because it is then the assumptions that are observing. (Bohm 2011, pp. 134 and 135*ff.*)

According to epistemological theory, there must be a greater distance away from the situation itself and movement toward the assumptions of the observer. Then it will be clear that "the possibility of an appropriate version of reality" (Pongratz 2010, p. 284), as proposed only by materialists and realists, cannot be substantiated. The actual question, however, is still excluded: what about the background assumptions of a supposedly objective logic for existence and those expressed by this fundamentalism.

There can be no other explanation for the destructive and sometimes polemic force with which some people engage in the dispute over reality. It seems more about opinions and assessments and less about clarifications. Any expectation of a self-observation of one's own belief structure or even tentative attempts to reflect on and perhaps reject the assumptions and show an openness to the plurality of scientific worldviews is in vain.

Like realists, the materialists believe they possess compelling and universally valid forms of knowledge; they simply exclude the assuming nature of their own forms of observation, perception, and evaluation and accuse others of being unreasonable.

Nothing else can explain why one of the most zealous representatives, Ludwig Pongratz, in his never-ending struggle against systemic-constructivist approaches, refers over and over again to the generally inconsequential dissertation by Ralf Nüse. Nüse claimed that the epistemological program of constructivism (cf. von Glasersfeld 1996) could be dismissed with the terse comment that "if you are unable to find access to your environment, then you will also not be able to determine that you have no access" (Nüse 1995, p. 251).

This comment has no substance, and it also applies in reverse: *If you assume your brain is creating accurate images of reality, you are unable to think that you may be unable to relate to it all.* Ultimately, you are unable to deal self-reflectively with evidence; eventually, the social constructions and their emotional anchoring are lost in a set of preexisting and preengaged concepts. You are not able to create a different picture of reality from the one always assumed.

Similarly, the materialists and neorealists cannot adequately deal with the coevolution of self-concerned brains, because they assume the relationship to be more open than it appears—according to everything that socially constructed evidence tells us. In its fundamentalist turn, the materialistic education theory deprives itself of an essential element of its own original appeal, namely, the possibility to draft a reality that enables the expression of other than the assumed mechanisms.

To recognize the unreal evidence does not mean opening the door for arbitrariness. Evidence can be recognized as long as it is viable, that is, it opens accessible pathways, although the criteria for evaluating accessibility are historically more variable than originally suspected. A look at the history of scientific errors is more than adequate to confirm this (cf. Zankl 2003, 2004).

This is not confined to the natural sciences but also applies to the humanities and the social sciences where objects are even more inaccessible to mathematic observation because they are constituted from tradition and interpretation—a logic that still exists in the exact sciences. Nevertheless, more than a temporary certitude and viability is not to be had considering the alternating exposure of observer and observed (cf. Arnold/Neuser 2017).

Added to this is the impossibility of an assumption-free observation—a fact that also applies to the aforementioned concept. It is hard to imagine anything could be more serious in this constructivist self-contradiction than the assertion that an observation creates an image of something that is.

Confirming this assumption of an image-creating observation with the nimbus of evidence, it becomes a teaching authority just as much as the all-knowing interjections of materialists and realists, who pretend to know what is "nonsense" while not noticing the simple fact that the way they have thought and written for three decades about education and training follows the unmistakable "I-want-to-remain-as-I-am" logic and remains blind to the possibilities of a changing world.

## NOTES

1. This quote is from the talk he gave at the Techonomy Conference in Lake Tahoe, California, USA (www.tomshardare.de/Internet-Universität, news-244471.html).
2. Weichert ultimately judges the potential of education's digital future only through the lens of classroom presence, omitting the fact that the best students do not always have to be at the same location, as the experience of Sebastian Thrun, pioneer of Stanford University's Massive Open Online Course (MOOC), clearly shows: Of the 160,000 students worldwide who participated in his MOOC, 23,000 passed the exam. None of the 248 students who achieved the top score of 100 percent was from Stanford. See the *New York Times* interview: http://wwwnytimep.com/2012/03/O5/education/moocs-large-courses-open-to-all-topple-campus-wallp.html.

*Chapter 3*

# Learning Is Not Mediated, but Appropriated

Learning takes the form of a seeking movement. It is always an expression of a person's *own* reasoning or *own* learning project. Imagine the example of a searchlight, whereby people spot *the* aspects of the learning subject that are most important to them and to which they can connect their prior knowledge and their own life experience.

The logic of a truly sustainable and lasting learning progress is not new, but the indications are always overlaid or pushed aside by didactic concepts that use quasi-military terms. The use of words like *intervention, control, conflict,* and *take over* are quite common, as if the use of such martial concepts alone could effectively conceal the obvious nature of many didactic failures. In this regard, a rational view can no longer ignore the facts

- People do not learn, although the facts are carefully presented and elaborately didacted.
- They do learn, although nothing was taught.
- They learn something different from what was taught.

However, not merely these obvious points show the limited effectiveness of didactic theory and practice. Systems theory has undeniably confronted the socio-scientific debate with the fact that successful change follows inside-out logic. This subject is the self-organization ("autopoiesis") of the living, where not just biological transformations but also social transformations supply a variety of visual material for consideration. In essence, although systems tend to remain as they are, they are also able to simultaneously adapt to changing environmental conditions by using them to create new and viable paths.

We cannot overlook the fact that many brain researchers today are presenting similar arguments when they point out that people in the learning process are mainly busy with themselves, or when asked the question whether it is possible to change themselves or others, the answer tends to be more negative than positive (cf. Roth 2007).

The criteria of self-centeredness always scores quite high: over 80 percent of the brain—according to some studies—is engaged in reusing elements that are already present when constructing new viable pathways. Other brain researchers report an even higher percentage and propose an operational cohesion of cognitive structures.

Whatever the percentage may be, the core didactic issue of how to effectively bring learners together with new knowledge and abilities remains unanswered. Surprisingly, we have to say that the traditional models continue to pretend that it is merely this 20 percent gap that somehow still allows the possibility for linear influences or for subject mediation.

Some didactic thinkers are beginning to distance themselves from such mediation illusions and have begun to develop didactics as a science of the *learner*. As such, it no longer turns merely on requirements or content structures, but rather tries to gain a deeper understanding of subjective conditions for an effective appropriation to take place, that is, the successful transformation of expanded knowledge and competence.

They provide an atmosphere of didactic humility, limited to an examination of the various possibilities for controlling the context for learning. They study each situational opportunity to support the individual search process and the change process. The fundamental didactic answer must turn away from the trance of average values, something that has been deterred by didactic research and theory development in the past, and actually face the singularity in appropriating knowledge and competence.

This movement is associated with a departure from the motivation theories and learning typologies routinely heard in the daily didactic discussion. These have ultimately proven to be useless attempts to save instructional or interventionist mediation concepts. In truth, they merely induce the educational practice of creating learners who appear to conform to a prefabricated image and cannot appear any other way than in the assigned form.

The shocking banality is the difference between intrinsic and extrinsic motivation. An obvious inside-outside distinction is used in systems theory, but in effect it is falsified by the interpretation "from the outside to the inside" which has very little to recommend it. Motivation originates from inner movements, similar to *emotions* (which, by the way, share the same etymological root in Latin *movere* = motion/to move).

The only conceivable answer to the singularity and the relative coherence of the appropriation movement of the learner is found in the didactic of context control: if we are unable to safely predict which environmental structures resonate with an individual learner and which do not, then we are left with only the diversity. To enable and support the appropriation process requires that we first and foremost provide useful context, diverse forms of content development, task management, and application opportunities.

This *enabling didactic strategy* (cf. Arnold et al. 2016) largely distances itself from the doctrine of control as it underlies the teaching concept of inner differentiation and focuses completely on the singularity of learner appropriation. Finally, we can hardly know with certainty what the learner has for inner connecting materials for constructing a learning object "from the inside out" and to effectively anchor it in the cognitive and emotional structures for use in competence development.

We are equally uncertain as to what forms of access the learners are able to use and what strategies and techniques of transformation and consolidation they already have. In conclusion, we usually have very little knowledge of the reinforcing or weakening experiences in their learning biography.

## EDUCATION AS APPLIED SELF-REFLECTION

The world is a system consisting of systems. These systems do not exist as independent systems separate from people. They emerge through observation, that is, through the manner in which you as an observer differentiate between what belongs in the system and what makes up your environment.

You can use the zoom: It is possible to systematically consider the organization of which you are a part, while also asking the question of how the various departments of the organization function as a system independently from one another. The lens widens from the narrow view of the classroom practice to focus rather on the entire organization as a cooperative enterprise and to thematize the organizational repercussions for possible implications on teaching.

Adult learning is another example viewed not only in the context of the adult educational institutions themselves, but also from the relationships of the target groups in the world of experience. The focus is on their learning practices as a lifelong worldview or their "lifeworld cognitive process" as Enno Schmitz already suggested in the 1980s (cf. Schmitz 1984). He anticipated a broad learning concept, which concerned not only the cognitive appropriation of new knowledge but the development of extended interpretations as well as the self-structuring of new questions and problems—interpretations, which now after twenty years are being reexamined in the discussions of competence.

The systems view of learning serves not merely the extended view of adult learning with its references to a lifeworld, but it also directs a differentiated view inward. The learners themselves are seen as units in the system, which in turn connect and interact more or less with different systems (e.g., cognitive or emotional). The cognitive systems "live" from the structures they have already constructed, and new things can be appropriated only within their own conditions, by testing the new on existing patterns and assimilating them (assimilation) or by adjusting a previously successful pattern, or even by giving up to enable you to rethink and understand (accommodation).

Jean Piaget (1896–1980) studied both mechanisms in detail (cf. Piaget 1981). Perhaps without realizing the full extent of his insights, Piaget thematized the learning form for fast-moving modern times. When learning is viewed as a circumstance of the lifeworld and education becomes increasingly related to lifetime experiences, learning through pattern breaking becomes the real form of lifelong learning. Its core mechanism is—guided—self-reflection.

The following self-check (table 3.1) is designed to help you track down these two mostly interwoven interactive learning movements in yourself. It

**Table 3.1.  The art of conscious accommodation (Arnold 2016, p. 27)**

*Self-Check:*
*Do you still subconsciously assimilate or have you learned to consciously accommodate? Suggestions for separating yourself from familiar viewpoints and reactions:*

| | |
|---|---|
| Assessment | - What is happening now? |
| | - What familiar responses are building in me? |
| | - Do I really want or need the consequences that could be? |
| Conflict avoidance | - What is being asked of me? |
| | - Can I appreciate the validity of the other person's perspective? |
| | - What other—surprising—response is possible on my part? |
| Construction | - What new interpretation can I accept? |
| | - What viewpoint must I change or give up? |
| | - What impact will it have on my life? |
| Openness | - How can I avoid clinging to my assessments? |
| | - How can I practice accepting differences? |
| | - How can I become more multifaceted? |
| Meditation | - How can I become more aware of my internal images and sensitivities? |
| | - Where do these come from? |
| | - How do I keep them there—where they belong? |
| Victimless endings | - Am I OK with acting like the victim? |
| | - How can I avoid this? |
| | - What can I do to help others avoid playing the role of the victim? |
| Deficit avoidance | - How can I avoid looking for deficiencies in others? |
| | - What are my own deficiencies? |
| | - How can I avoid making subsequent interpretations and actions? |

may increase your awareness of your own imprisonment in familiar patterns of perception and reactions. Although this may not break the rigid power of habit, at least it has been brought into focus, and in the future, your approach to observation will no longer be so straight on, but will also keep your own way of observing in the peripheral sight.

Such self-reflection is an activity performed by an observer trying to understand the systemic functions to which he or she is subject, but also those that emanate from within. Self-reflection enables the observer to consciously realize that his or her actions are not merely intentional, but also functional. Thoughts, emotions, and actions fulfill functions we are not aware of, as we are a "master of our own house" only in a limited way. Similarly, we cannot know the effects our actions trigger in other systems. Namely, there are also functional reactions, that is, the efforts to remain "faithful" to functions successfully fulfilled in the past.

## UNAVOIDABLE SIDE EFFECTS

The findings of systems researchers tell us that systems cannot be effectively influenced although we continue to try. Most intervention concepts are sub-complexes, which is also true for didactic concepts and recommendations. They often overlook the self-organizing power of the systems at which they are directed and seldom have a strategy for dealing with unwanted side effects. These are seen as unpleasant companion aspects, not as an unavoidable reaction to context that functions according to a different logic. Consequently, we accept the following

- Teaching often has only a transparent and fleeting influence.
- People can know a lot and still be unable to do anything.
- Forgetting also seems to be part of learning.
- Long stays at educational institutions show undesired as well as desired effects (e.g., fatigue and inner resignation of the learners).

As systems research teaches, because we fundamentally cannot limit the effect of an intervention to only the desirable effects, every problem solution achieved is usually the starting point for the emergence of new problems. The painstakingly achieved effects are simultaneously the cause of new disruptions to the system and new processes of settling and balancing for the overall situation.

Permanent solutions are unrealistic as they are unsystematic. Numerous warlike involvements clearly illustrate that successful intervention and the fall of dictatorships do not lead to peace as interventionists had hoped. Rather, the resulting power vacuum enables new forces to spread and to sow chaos anew throughout the entire system—in some cases, in more dramatic practice than even the original reason for the intervention.

On a smaller context, we have to deal with the unwanted side effects of our well-intentioned and even well-planned actions. Managers, for example, can write a book about how, because of resistance in the system, they are forced to restate, re-justify, and renegotiate their targets and their projects. If they make the mistake of meeting the system head on with increased resistance, they run the risk of running the whole ship aground.

Instead of "downshifting" and entering a phase of reflection to study the "good reasons" behind the resistance encountered, most try to "break" the opposition down with "more of the same" (cf. Watzlawick 1988). If they fail, the explanations of the cause and the accusations of guilt are quickly on hand.

Many managers even think that their lack of success may have something to do with them not being decisive enough or not doing enough. Similarly, "more of the same" strategies can be observed in the field of education

- The growing uncertainty about the educational issues of the future is being met with detailed planning and complex concepts for monitoring results and quality assurance.
- Equally decisive are educational concepts that hold the belief that the supposedly increasing lack of discipline among the youth can be met with traditional concepts of a disciplinary pedagogy.
- Ultimately, even the indications of the shortening half-life of knowledge have not lead to any fundamental questioning of teaching methods and the strategies of handling knowledge, but rather to pleas for the preservation and intensification of past practice.

Often, such routine explanations are inspired by mechanical models of social interaction, where effects are attributed solely to the input of energy and the operation of the proper switches at the right times. In such cases, a wrong notion leads to a wrong action, which cannot be made "more correct" or "more legitimate" through stubborn repetition or forced continuation. It remains a desperate attempt to force an outcome that often fizzles out as a ridiculous gesture. Usually, the players realize only too late that they have violated a fundamental rule of systemic change.

---

**TEXTBOX   3.1**

Treat the system or the actors in it, respectfully and with appreciation, while justifying your own change interests and meshing them with the traditional routines and possibilities of the other actors.

---

Unintended side effects are unavoidable, yet they can be calculated in advance and planned into management or mediation activities.[1] People who are aware of the social resistance are more open and less determined, even when pursuing clear targets. In the interest of achieving their own goals, they take into account the concerns and thoughts of other members of the system and try—*also* or *primarily!*—to develop the intervention on the basis of their procedural logic.

Such a procedure is based on a different philosophy of design and control. This philosophy is not merely soundly based in systems theory but is also more modern. Workers in a democratic society no longer want to just obey and carry out what someone else orders. They want to interact as equals and bring in their experience and have their competence respected. Authoritarian or interventionist concepts always activate, understandably, a *system defense*.

Peter Heintl and Ewald E. Krainz made use of the term "system defense" as early as 1994, to describe the well-established, often latent, but totally effective ability of organizations to ward off change. Such resistance illustrates

> the extent to which organizational processes can become "self-running," in such a way that it is often impossible for control efforts to interrupt these "auto-piloted" processes. Furthermore, the control efforts themselves become part of the "auto-programs" trapped in the dynamics of the organizational apparatus. (Heintl/Krainz 1994, p. 164)

This implies that attempts that appear to deny problems or the need for change, even to the point of viewing them as "biased" or associating them with the dark forces of the "guilty ones," not only counteract lasting change, but they also reveal much about the working mechanizations of the system and its openness to deal with requirements in a new way. For example, when executives take an "it's up to fate!" position or practice a blind and ineffective activism, it can be seen as an initial indication that development processes at the competence and personality levels are needed.

The same holds for the unnecessary complication of a concern for change, which on closer inspection, only serves to satisfy their self-need for some causality or to get so self-entangled only to leave everything as it was. It is a self-deception when things appear "disarmingly clear" (ibid., p. 187), and it is very difficult to think otherwise about it. In seeking the possibilities for overcoming such system defenses, we cannot find any unless a meaningful self-reflection and an effective self-transformation takes place.

As long as they do not seem to be able to discern how they are deceiving themselves, any interest in change is futile. Managers and executives have a large part to play. It is their job to "install reflection" (ibid., p. 190), which means they are to create possibilities and opportunities for strategic thinking, questioning, and communicating with their team members and employees. A learning enterprise is characterized by whether the people who work there are consistently thinking of their own system defenses.

In the absence of social science expertise, such self-reflection on the part of the management cannot succeed, especially in the teaching-learning process. Social systems do not function on a technical-economic basis, but perhaps primarily on social mechanisms. The *Challenger* shuttle craft tragedy could as well have been caused by a communications and leadership failure, just as the ongoing crisis over the manipulation of the diesel engines by Volkswagen in 2015.

Social scientific know-how and personality formation are not only important in making teams more successful in their cooperation and communication. These competencies have actually become a success factor in technical problem solving. The idea, still frequently encountered, that the social sciences are useful aids for "the business" while the major viewpoints continue to be shaped by business economics and the engineering disciplines is not only outdated, but actually harmful.

On the contrary, it is essential to understand, especially, for economic and technical success, that people always act on the basis of what they think is true and correct, even when referring to what they believe is evidence. This is particularly obvious in the management and structure of organizations: these are shaped by stories, traditions, and established "game rules," which can be overlooked if considering only organizational charts and policy regulations.

If an outsider, such as a consultant, is told of a business problem, it matters who is describing the problem and what group interests could be the basis for that particular perspective on the issues, namely, what makes the problem into a problem in the first place. These are the specific forms of describing, weighting, and commenting. Informal storytelling not only reveals the range of interests, but also gives context to the self-management forces and routines at work.

Systems do not always react when exposed to new facts emerging after an analysis; rather, spontaneous reactions and interpretations provide insight into their experiences or how similar situations were managed in the past. Problems are good opportunities to gain a better understanding of the organization.

Organizations have the tendency to continue their histories, and exactly for that reason, management can only develop the business when that history is known and understood. That history can be redirected only when management realizes that people do not only react (or not all in the first place) to external stimuli, but are also bound to traditional interpretations and their own inner structures.

These abilities to navigate the tribal world of the company and ultimately shape effective innovation imply a networking capability, since the executives who are able to socially embed their expertise have to "accept different viewpoints" (Gomez/Probst 1995, p. 28*ff.*). They must be able, similar to the social scientists, to recognize not just *first-order reality* (= "what the object is"), but rather they frequently have to deal with perspectives of a second-order reality (= "what the meaning of the object is for me").

Professional social scientists are effective only if they can link the two together while enabling something new to arise as explained in the book *Surviving in the Simultaneity: Leadership in the TBD Organization* by organizational consultant Susanne Ehmer and others:

> Management in the TBD organization develops an intelligent approach for differentiating between the known and unknown. It does not deceive itself and others with certitudes where there are none, but in its place, substitutes leading questions. At periodic intervals, they and their organizations are supplied with external perspectives (customers, consultants, cells of unconventional thinkers), so as to be able to see and realize what was (previously) not seen and realized. This facilitates a dynamic balance between using proven routines and successful experience and the search for new; opens the view to what routines have merely a braking effect and where these brakes could be loosened or if new ones need to be installed if the tempo becomes too risky. (Ehmer et al. 2016, p. 59)

Successful "managers of the TBD organization" (ibid.) know that the changes take place in the head and not as a result of inspired interventions—at least not in a systemically compatible and truly sustainable form. They also know that not learning is mostly an art (cf. Simon 1999) that actors practice for years to form and perfect, having acquired routines that they seek to preserve even though hardly ever able to achieve the desired results with them—an urge for continuity with consequences. At any rate, the actors have sustainably learned to no longer learn.

## INDEPENDENT STUDY: THE LOGIC IN THE ACT OF SEEKING

The concept of the searching movement is an old one. Originally coined by Alexander Mitscherlich (1996, p. 24), it points out the self-inclusion in all long-term effective learning: "The constant is the act of appropriation, not the content appropriated" (ibid., p. 24). It is the search, selection, decoding, testing, and the reconstruction and deepened understanding that transform the individual and find expression of the altered abilities to deal with the self and others.

According to Alexander Mitscherlich, such a search can merely *attempt*, "to escape from the illusions about the world, about others, and, most of all, about myself" (ibid., p. 24*ff.*). The effort can be successful only if independently performed on your own. Instruction and curricula and even the standardization and management of this movement would already undermine the concept from the start. Why is that? Because it requires ownership and an "enabling environment" from the start (Meyer et al. 2008, p. 1). It is all about facilitating a context that indirectly enables the learner to plan the searching movements.

Hans Tietgens introduced the term "search movement" to the German education discourse in the 1980s, linking the term to the concept of self-study. This concerns a careful self-reflection and the balance for your own potential with the social expectations, which can only be developed through your own search:

> Out of all the diversity that once appeared possible to the individual, a certain pattern of life emerges. It leads to connections and consolidations as we adopt the roles. Some of these bonds are imposed, while others are decided by individual commitment. Yet, even these decisions between different social reward systems are mostly not a free choice. Adults are expected to honor such decisions and, in this way, to guarantee a minimum level of assured behaviors. (Tietgens 1986, p. 91)

The paradox of the curriculum vitae is that although these "assured behaviors" are the objective of every teaching-learning process, the achievement of this objective still requires shaping of uncertainty and the use of creative freedoms.

The search movement spoken of by Mitscherlich and Tietgens is, on closer inspection, really a "trying" movement. It sometimes needs help to succeed. It requires access to options and irritation and support. These two dimensions—irritation and support—characterize what makes the process of personality formation successful in the context of independent learning (cf. Arnold/Lermen 2013). They are based on self-reflection—knowing that you do not have the truth about yourself, "You search for it and are discontented all of your life" (ibid., p. 25).

This discontent cannot be removed by didactics or doctrine since it necessarily remains rooted in the logic of certitude and finding, something that requires working through uncertainties and continued searching. "The educated boor is as uneducated as the one who knows nothing" (ibid.), wrote Alexander Mitscherlich in orienting us on his thesis of modern education that ultimately aims at personality formation. Education, for Mitscherlich, is the expression of a "search movement and, increasingly, a coordinated search. It must lift itself out if it becomes mired in an examination of inaccessible, self-assured 'knowledge.' Dogma means the end of education" (Mitscherlich, 1996, p. 25).

The search movement requires independent learning. This thrives when the participants have sufficient opportunity to take their concerns, questions, learning projects, and perspectives as the starting point for their search and clarifications—framed by an arrangement and accompanied by a learning assistant. The latter also aims to initiate the "search movements" but is aware of the fact that this is only possible if done with a restrained manner, which results in very specific requirements for professional educators. Tietgens wrote:

> It is all about the ability to see into the interpretations of the situation, which are affected by the constellation of professional conditions. The pressure to perform can sometimes leave the impression that clever communications are the most appropriate means for tackling a problem. A problem-oriented supply of argumentation is indeed indispensable, otherwise planning becomes undone in the occasional. It would be difficult to implement something corresponding to the situation if it presents more complex requirements. (Tietgens 1986, p. 43)

This formulation highlights the abilities—professional abilities—required by an independent learning counselor, yet not automatically acquired by completing an academic degree. Learning assistants need self-reflection as much as they need professional knowledge. At the core, however, is the importance attached to the knowledge by the professional and their own de facto ability to deal with a lack of knowledge.

What is needed is an attitude—fed from the insight of knowing that we don't (cannot) know—that remains in the search mode while appreciating another's searching movements and strengthening their resources. Just as an education snob is truly not educated, the "knowing" learning assistant is hardly able to assist another's search movement. "Knowing" lives from the delusion of completeness. This is an allusion to the "state of having found." Learning assistants must be able to adapt professionally to situations of searching and not finding. Professionalism is based on a "seeker attitude" (ibid., p. 49), not a "having-found attitude."

The ability to hold this attitude is an expression of deep tranquility. The professional learning assistant cannot be irritated by a premature diagnosis or impatience with regard to the aim or the path of the ongoing process. On the contrary, they are able to control their own restlessness and focus on the here-and-now of the process. In this context, dispensing with old habits of perception—both cognitive and emotional—is of fundamental importance. Only by achieving this are they capable of letting the world come to them;

not always seeing the new as another version of the familiar and they can let themselves be surprised.

## NOTE

1. The term "mediation" refers to the professional effort to pass on to the next generation a certain level of expertise-knowledge-skills, something not as easily accomplished as the common term suggests. You cannot "impart" (in the sense of mediate) competence, anymore than you can "pass it on." According to the current argument—we can arrange content in a way that the learner has the opportunity to let the brain do what only the brain can do: that is, independently appropriate knowledge and abilities, with the support and advice of experts, able to call in their expertise but not forced to do so.

*Chapter 4*

# We Learn from Others, but We Think Alone

People are each other's mutual learning environment. They reveal the world, explaining and illustrating as they arrange the "classroom" for new experiences. Special forms of discovery, dialog, documentation, and guided observations and evaluations are intended to facilitate the systematic appropriation of knowledge and abilities so that novices can acquire expertise and improve their performance.

This describes the input side of the teaching-learning relationship, which features a choice of didactics, reduction, and illustration. Included are the school buildings, textbooks, lesson plans, and teacher training strategies, all to serve the same goal of providing the optimal context for the learning event.

Whether, and in what way, learners are able to actually benefit from these arrangements, however, is written on another page. The brain functions separately and independently from these arrangements. The mechanisms of confrontation, appropriation, and new formation in the brain change when in an organized situation or even a teaching-learning relationship, but also because it is their nature to function that way, as they have functioned over thousands of years

- First, we have to acknowledge the fact that it is human thinking, feeling, and acting that create the circumstances. People can articulate and provide information about what and why they do something. In doing so, they are open to other interpretations and explanations, which they can evaluate, compare, and accept, if—according to their own view—the other action holds greater promise.
- The human brain is primarily busy with itself throughout this process; in other words, it can only sort and appropriate competencies that already have a lot to be said for them. The brain is a connecting tissue, that is, constantly

occupied in achieving a meaningful balance between the processing of the own possible interpretations and the "distractions" it encounters from the outside. The brain is constantly creating the learner's plausible experience, which is why we tend to stick with what is familiar, rather than following the "facts."

- Brains "learn" by interacting with the learner's emotions: the difference between cognition and emotion is merely an analytical view; in the learning process itself, both work in unison. Much evidence suggests that restrictive, frightening, or even offensive experiences hinder rather than promote sustainable appropriation and competence development. All that is critical for the success of the learning process is the learner's own feelings of self-empowerment, which are strengthened by constructive learning experiences. It can truly be said that this is the motor of the learning ability and the will to learn.

The idea of *the loneliness of the brain in the learning process* emphasizes the fact that no long-term effects of the learning processes (e.g., retention and ability) can be attained unless there is a conscious and deliberate *self-movement* by the learner. All learning is independent or self-directed, as clearly shown from the worldwide experience with distance learning as well as informal learning (on the job, exposure to media, etc.).

People have the power to acquire complex competencies completely outside of the institutionalized classroom and deliver convincing proof of the power of experience itself. They are doing something they are not entitled to do. The logic of our current system of authorization does not allow for it! Successful competence building does not correlate with the tightly supervised learning process, but rather with the intensity of the experience of self-empowerment, self-direction, and self-responsibility—the basic substances often invoked for lifelong learning.

In contrast, the graduates of supervised learning processes often experience far too little training in these substances; in fact, a twenty-year socialization in the context of expected teaching has largely alienated them from their own learning energies. The brain is not only lonely, but it is exhausted.

What could be closer to the educating effect of experience than to support its increased expression in prearranged, institutionalized classrooms

- instead of dosing out learning units (for example, teaching hours or lectures), arrange long-term learning processes;
- instead of attendance control, guide and enable self-structured learning phases with self-controls; and
- instead of adapting to intentions, create diverse opportunities for independent self-development of clearly written social expectations as described by standards and competence profiles.

Such advanced development of institutionalized education would simultaneously account for the currently observable limitations (= overcome the familiar restrictions and rules) while being driven *also* but not entirely by the spread and use of digital media. The universal presence of technology allows an outreach logic that facilitates access to knowledge, application assistance, and practice, all while reformulating the unavoidable question: What location is required for sustainable learning?

However, the *loneliness of the brain* is not meant to imply that the social phases of encounter and exchange are no longer essential conditions for sustainability. The opposite is the case: the cognitive-emotional totality of an effective appropriation can only be expressed in phases where these coexist. The mere collection of topics is not sufficient. This applies, in particular, to methods where the self-learning abilities are merely assumed and not directly targeted for support.

Above all else, it is important to recognize and evaluate each learner's current self-learning ability and to intentionally promote it (through the exercise of learning methods, increasingly complex problem solving, etc.) in order to meet the demands of what is de facto happening: the appropriation movement, principally, in a solitary brain.

## CHANGE HAPPENS IN THE MIND

Philosophy and the social sciences throughout history have repeatedly had to recall that *the* reality does not exist; rather there are, more or less, interpretations of an evidence-based nature. Correspondingly, there is no completeness. Everything is a social construction and even the experts, who are in position to know what knowledge belongs in the realm of problem-solving competence, can only toss their own expertise onto the balance scales—reality is not immediately shared even with them.

Not all people perceive the most concrete problems, entanglements, and complications in the same way; this also applies to the experts. What they are able to realize also depends on what they are used to realizing, even if all others contradict them and agree, for example, that the issue is a "real" problem; they may view it merely as a question to be answered or, perhaps, an irritation.

This constructivism and dependency on the interpretation of worldviews is still unfamiliar to many, and they get entangled with their partners, friends, or colleagues and find themselves in a never-ending battle for reality. They hold fast to what seems to them to be the case and have not yet really understood that without shared views and meanings as well as an openness to the interpretations of others, there can be no successful individual learning, nor organizational learning. The reason is:

---

**TEXTBOX   4.1**

Change begins in the head. Generally, an innovation is already "half implemented" in their own minds before the participants are fully aware of it.

---

However, the first step occurs when the responsible people (e.g., executives, teachers, consultants) see themselves as "responsible interpreters" by living, understanding, and increasingly learning that their views, their projects, and their explanations are only their "constructions." The "taming of the view" (Schmidt 1998) is just as much of a requirement for successful management, consulting, and support as the "interdependency of the view" (Arnold/Siebert 2006).

Only such a systemic-constructivist attitude provides access to the professional competence needed to respond deliberately to others and, rather than lecturing, allowing the co-construction of reality to take place. The biographical experiences, early emotional instincts, and self-competence of the other person serve, namely, as the inner basis for a sustainable transformation of their competence profile.

In particular, executives are encouraged to "take care" to involve the individual in shaping the workstation, the department, and the operations. It is no longer enough that the individual learns and regularly participates in training events. Questions must be asked about the operating conditions: in what way can the colleagues and the business "learn" from the use or sharing of what is learned? Organizational learning is not focused on the content, but rather on improving and routinely applying common abilities and successfully learning how to deal with new and complex challenges.

The familiar focus on designing the "solid" organizational framework conditions fades—but in no way, does it lose its overall importance—as the "soft" factors of interpretation and meaning move to prominence in the joint undertaking. At the forefront now are the everyday understandings and "theories in use" by the members of the organization, in other words, the routine patterns in which the social context reveals itself. The aim of organizational learning is

1. to raise awareness,
2. to reflect on the shared meanings and visions of the routines and strategies in everyday operations, and
3. to transform by initiating the appropriate learning process, for example, by replacing the destructive or crippling or futile forms of communication with proactive, energy-packed—visionary—as well as cooperative forms of dialog.

---

**TEXTBOX   4.2**

Based on underlying conviction, companies as well as societies overall experience sustained growth only when the shared knowledge base, that is, the entirety of their shared meanings, viewpoints, and patterns, is continuously and intentionally further developed, and along the way, the tried and tested patterns are disrupted.

---

"Learning" becomes "cultural development," in other words, the further development of socially shared worldviews. The organizational learning processes change, generate, and develop common forms of symbolism, patterns of expression, and even collective visions. The recent impulses in teaching and learning as well as findings from brain research are changing and expanding the didactic concept of many teachers.

The fundamental ideas of nearly every didactic model that knowledge and competence can be imparted and the central role of the teacher in the learning process are being challenged. The emerging evidence cannot be ignored simply to avoid questioning past didactic thinking. The demolishing of traditional ideas is nevertheless required before new—professional—forms of teaching-learning cooperation and the design of framework conditions and organizational structures can begin to take root.

## THE INTRANSITIVE NATURE OF SKILL DEVELOPMENT

The development of "multidimensional education theory" (VbW 2015) refers to the effort to account for the intransitive nature of competence development. The dominance of one dimension—namely the curriculum content—recedes, focusing instead on the *experienced* and the often-overlooked emotional "substance" of sustainable appropriation and transformation of competency.

Taking the cautious view of the emergent from an event is fundamental just as it was also basic in the enabling didactic from its beginnings in the 1990s (cf. Arnold 1997). This initial tentative attempt to redefine the interrelationship of teaching and learning as well as that of content and individual—beyond the reductionist-mechanistic instinct didactic—first triggered surprise and vehement criticism of the underlying constructivist thesis.

The discourse sometimes took on the character of a dispute over reality, often overlooking the efforts of brain researchers to understand the person's thinking, feeling, and acting were increasingly starting from a constructivist interpretation of the autopoietic cohesion of the underlying processes.

---

**TEXTBOX   4.3**

The acceptance level of the constructivist thesis has been increasing in recent years. The acceptance grew when faced with the indisputable view that it was no longer possible to completely overlook the autonomy of the learner in the context of the autopoiesis of consciousness (German: *Autopoiesis des Bewusstseins*) (Luhmann 2005).

---

This fundamentally changed the role of the parties in the teaching-learning process and suggested a loosely structured link between teaching and learning. The learners' maturing competency initially appeared to follow internal standards and took place—even without any, or in spite of, forced didactic intervention.

The *self-directed competency* of the learner in the constitutive significance of the learning movement and competence profile was the increasingly shared view. People began to understand that these movements could be encouraged and even initiated, but not guaranteed by an open but also diverse arrangement of appropriative contexts.

The *enabling didactic* developed more and more into a theory of *self-directed learning and skills development*. Similarly, the argument inspired by recent brain physiology studies suggests that the relationship between teaching and learning is more intransitive by nature. In this sense, Gerald Hüther wrote about this human ability in his book *Mit Freude lernen—ein Leben lang*:

> To reconcile the disruption of the internal order caused by changes in the external environment by enabling certain internally stored response patterns. This refers to an action that is individually initiated through the person's own actions. (Hüther 2016, p. 28)

Hüther did not restrict himself to the prevailing models of regulated learning, but rather traced the learner-focused learning theory (cf. Holzkamp 1993), albeit without realizing for himself what trodden path he was following. He concluded, "Only things that have significance to the learner can be learned" (ibid., p. 41).

This was a replication of what Klaus Holzkamp proposed in the 1990s, namely, a deep understanding of the learning movement is not possible unless the learner is asked to name "a sound reason for action in his/her vital interest" (Holzkamp 1991, p. 27). This freed the concept of learning from its objectifying external view and began the discourse about the inner forms of expression and the mechanisms for successful skills development.

This view considers the obvious fact that learning represents a *structured appropriation movement by the learner*, where the direction, dynamic, and sustainability are inseparable from previous routines and experiences of self-management. Every transformation permitted and carried out by the learner is a movement within the framework of previous strategies to take and shape unforeseen events. It is a way of embracing "the uncertainty, since there is no more certainty" (Ehmer et al. 2016, p. 20), or perhaps, there never was any.

Learning requires an open attitude, at least partially, as it also serves opening and strengthening of the identity as it constantly seeks to go beyond its boundaries. In this sense, successful learning is more like a self-structured experiment than a guided enlightenment—similar to the familiar "Parable of the Butterfly":

> One day there appeared a small opening in the cocoon; a man sat and watched the butterfly for several hours, as it struggled to squeeze its body through the tiny hole. Then, suddenly, it appeared to be exhausted and stopped moving. It seemed as if it had come as far as it could, but could go no further on its own strength. So, the man decided to help the butterfly: He took a pair of scissors and cut open the cocoon, leaving an easy path for the butterfly to completely emerge.
>
> But something was not as it should be when the butterfly emerged. Its body was wrinkled and small, its wings were shriveled. The man continued to watch it, hoping that at any moment it would spread its lovely wings and fly away. But, none of that happened. Instead, the butterfly spent the rest of its life weak and puny, dragging around its shriveled wings. It was never able to fly.
>
> What the man in his kindness and eagerness never understood was that the restrictive cocoon and the struggle necessary to get through the opening was nature's way of forcing fluids from the butterfly's body into its wings. In this way, it would be ready for flight soon after it gained its freedom from the cocoon. Sometimes, struggles are exactly what we need in our lives. If we could go through life with no obstacles, we would be cripples. We would never be as strong as we could be and never able to fly and achieve our destiny. (Steinbach 2016, p. 68)

The story clearly illustrates what the primary aim of the enabling didactic of accompanying the learning process and what competence development should be: reinforcing learner development—not intervention for the sake of intervention. This may be prescribed in the curricula or well-intended, but it can also preempt learners' self-development or even hinder or harm it.

The danger is present, in particular, if the teaching is all too easily connected to the learning, indeed as mentioned earlier, when the former is interpreted and conceived as a prerequisite and condition for the latter. This stems from a mental short circuit or, as Klaus Holzkamp suggested, a "teach-learn short circuit,"[1] which occurs not because it actually was proven after trial to be the causal factor, but because we are accustomed to assuming that it is so.

Nietzsche would say: "We still have our eye, our psychology set on it" (Nietzsche 1972, p. 51). Other forms of expression come much closer to the enabling didactic learning concept in describing the relationship between teaching and learning: for example, the Polish word for learning (*uczyc sie*) carries a connotative meaning much like "teach yourself, learn yourself," which as a reflexive verb corresponds more to an intransitive reading of the teaching-learning relationship.

As stated earlier, "to learn" is, incorrectly, *not* an intransitive verb. It presupposes an object, although there is none—at least of a type and form reserved for subjective logic or learning rationale, one that learners can relate to the object of learning. The possible learning outcomes depend on the subjective searching and appropriation movements, which have to be conceived and shaped separately from the expectation of teaching effectiveness associated with the content.

Consequently, a *learner focus* is merely a first step in enabling teaching-learning process, especially since much still remains rhetorically. The continuation and in-depth understanding is found in an *outcome-oriented* approach, which documents, acknowledges, and earmarks the emerging learning outcomes and skills as an expression of self-structured appropriation. Not only the hype surrounding informal learning has sharpened the gaze onto what actually happens when learners are able to highlight and demonstrate their skills: *Learners always follow an "inside-out" learning logic, in that they appropriate competencies that were never intended or solve problems that they previously had no way of solving.*

Such news clearly gave the EU a reason to produce another frame of reference, the European Qualifications Framework (EQF). The framework is intended to shift the focus in "a departure from the traditional systems which emphasize the learning inputs (length of experience, type of institution)"[2]— a major, if not revolutionary, change to the framework in order to ensure a rational consideration of the competencies of the individual.

To what extent this rationality will find expression in the establishment of more transparent and more accessible higher education system as well as a certification system that recognizes competencies and certifies competence is not yet clear. It is also impossible to predict what will become of content and uniform curricula, when the monopoly of the institutions, the guardians of knowledge, is breached to allow more flexible forms of proof of competence, for example, those that allow a Joschka Fischer, or another informal learner, to obtain accreditation and certification for "equivalent" competencies.

Because institutions protect their content, the issue is still how much institutionalization and institutional diversity really needs a "multi-option education and training system" in order to develop and certify *the* competencies increasingly merged in the competence debate under the heading "personality development." The Bavarian Industry Association (German: *Vereinigung der*

*Bayerischen Wirtschaft* (VbW)) stated in its 2015 "Education: More Than Specialization" review:

> Large segments of society are now aware that securing a viable employment system for the future as well as a high quality of life requires much more skillful management than was the case fifteen years ago. . . .
>
> People in such a society can only achieve their potential and the good life if they are equipped with a personality structure beyond just their knowledge and skills, one which provides them not merely with safe behaviors but also the willingness and ability to shape their own lives and to participate in the social challenges—also on a global scale. (VbW 2015, p. 9)

The issue of self-directed competence development pushes the role of the learner to the forefront of didactic thinking. Transformation depends on learners increasingly becoming aware of their own authorship, without which, at best a "defensive" but hardly an "expansive" learning can be expected (Holzkamp 1993).

Expansive learning follows a primitive human ability to self-organize and to "embrace uncertainty" (Ehmer et al. 2016, p. 20). This ability is paralyzed by low stimulus context, where accepting and adapting traditions is the primary goal—didactic claims that reflect not only a mechanistic-linear way of thinking, but also the continuation of authoritarian forms educating the next generation. These not only have a nonlinear and mechanistic effect on what they set out to achieve, but they are also able to paralyze.

The common sarcastic critique of teachers, "Come into my classroom, where you will not find any self-structuring," confirms an unintended side effect of this impossible didactic, not a failure of an intervention strategy. Brain-physiological studies show that children learn how to switch to a kind of sleep mode during their time in school, whereas after school they can switch back to an excitable mode for learning (cf. Spitzer 2007), which illustrates the giant paradox in the instructional pedagogy for self-development.

This paradox is unavoidable. We cannot overlook the growing evidence revealed by modern research on the brain and competence as well as on systemic intervention, especially, as there is no justification for "more of the same."

---

**TEXTBOX 4.4**

Our educational institutions must be transformed to places of self-structured learning, where diverse approaches for the appropriation and evaluation of competencies are offered in a climate conducive to appreciation and encounter.

An enabling, situation-oriented position for the creation and support of the teaching-learning process avoids the use of terms that are not suitable for an understanding of what is involved in dealing with what may be the "autopoiesis of cognition" (Luhmann 2005) in the subject system.

A situation-oriented didactic strives to redefine the "pedagogic order," which marks a complex arrangement, inviting to self-structured appropriation. Special "learning architectures and online learning platforms" (Arnold et al. 2016) open suitable new options as well as a professionalism, which at its core provides systemic learning support and program guidance. Such contexts are not predictable, but are rather optional in their effect. They emphasize the self-movements of the learner and avoid every hope of efficiency in order to enable some effectiveness to emerge in the first place.

## EXPERIENCE: PERSONALITY DEVELOPMENT AS AN EMOTIONAL TRANSFORMATION

If we define *personality development* as the act of performing *self-reflection, sober review, and prudent and socially embedded actions*, the question follows as to what we actually know about the formation of such actions. The scope of this book prevents a detailed analysis of all the research and theories on development and the formation of identity and competence, but the findings can be condensed down to a thesis that proposes that change, in the sense of patterns for sustainable change, is possible.

However, this presupposes experience in dealing with forms of self-reflection (cf. Siebert 2011). The habitual practice of these forms is increasingly seen as the core of a mature personality. The core dimensions of such a reflective education strategy are:

- an "applied cognitive theory" (cf. Arnold 2011),
- a consideration of the "emergent" in new assignment structures, and
- a conscious involvement in diachronic and synchronic systems that act as a network of assurances.

If we are to change, we must recognize and accept the difference. But what forces are we to follow once we decide for a change? Humberto Maturana has repeatedly reminded us of our obligation to "confess the recognition" (Maturana, cited in Pörksen 2008, p. 70). He wrote:

All knowledge is necessarily observer-dependent, claims of an absolute reality tempt terror. . . . What does it mean . . . to label something as right or wrong? Is a hypothesis proven correct when it fits to what I believe? Am I willing to listen and believe something merely because the so-called evidence agrees with my own presumptions? Can I label something as false if it is not in harmony with my own version? Is something ever per se right or wrong? What criteria does a person use to accept a premise as proof? (ibid., p. 83)

It is the job and the aim of *reflective education* to tune in to such questions and assist the learners in the formation of an opinion characterized less by knowledge than by searching. It is observing the observation that is the fundamental element in personality formation and organizational development. Reflectively managed organizations know:

Failing to communicate about the observation of perceptions made by employees and managers, means there can be no proper control. . . . The central management function is to observe what happens to the observations, how are they communicated and interpreted, to what decisions and actions do they lead, and how are these received. (Ehmer et al. 2016, p. 42*ff.*)

Reflective management is used to cultivate various interpretations of current situational assessments, and they are practiced in the forms of cooperation to see that "different perspectives, experiences, and interests can lead to different observations and assessments" (ibid., p. 45). Such openness does not imply that everything is completely relative or that "anything goes" as is sometimes feared. Rather, it is about the professional *value* to protect the questioning, the searching, and the attempts, while never being subject to disposition itself (for who would saw off the branch of opportunity for free thinking and evidence-based critique of situations on which they are sitting).

This normative attitude also includes "civilized contempt" (Strenger 2015). The inevitable norms of a civilized society in no way contradict the systemic-constructivist observation theory. The theory depends much more on the fact that cognition and shaping of open-mindedness requires, paradoxically, a normative contextualization that "ideally, is counterfactual," as stated by Kersten Reich (2002, p. 102):

Constructivists cannot help but to defend speaking out against merely egoistic, profitable for some, interesting for a few, or meaningful claims as being a social process, united under claims of equality. If constructivists did not do this, then those who would first eliminate constructivism, those who would then be allowed to keep their not so open version of reality (e.g., elitist, group-egoistic, politically one-sided, etc.) as the ultimate justification and implement it as a universal norm. (ibid., p. 104)

Overcoming of our own learned patterns of thinking, feeling, and acting requires reflection and an ultimate acknowledgement that observers develop in specific biographic and worldly contexts in which they test and consolidate their worldviews, while learning to interpret the world in ways they are able to tolerate. Their beliefs are a resistant fabric that they learn to rely on.

Any transformation of their own preferred patterns of emotional and cognitive constructions of reality, however, cannot succeed without seeing through the fateful randomness of the origins of their own beliefs. The "unconscious interlacing" of beliefs must be made "visible and insightful within the soul of the family" (Schneider 2016, p. 24) so that the interlacing can be seen, relativized, and overcome in order to create "new possibilities of feeling, thinking, and acting and cooperating with one another" (ibid., p. 25) as the sculpturing approach of systemic families and organizational therapies tries to achieve.

In the process, participant learning is principally seen as an open event, started and supported as a learning project. This approach initially gives learners an interest in the topic—a step that is often surprising and sometimes met with rejection. Especially, at the beginning when they slip into the familiar role of a passive vessel and find it hard to take seriously, many participants ask, "Why should I say what skill I want to acquire here?" Teachers find it hard to start the teaching-learning process with them and their skeptical attitudes.

The enabling didactic, in the ideal case, starts on the basis of specifically defined skill profiles that have been standardized by the education policy or by important contractors and client systems, knowing that the mere existence of these standards does not justify switching to the naive "transfer mode" simply because it is a familiar tradition. Susanne Kraft rightly states:

> If learning is primarily defined through the individual and not through the situation and knowledge is conceived as an individual construction, then "transferring knowledge" strictly speaking, is impossible through instruction and teaching. At the very least, it is not possible to create a specific instruction that directly insures that learners will be able to demonstrate after a certain time some desired behavior. (Kraft 2006, p. 209)

Admittedly, teaching is not merely instructional. The didactic forms have always been loaded with numerous activities that are concerned with effectively linking the know-how to be acquired with the learner's possibilities and past experiences. Such efforts do not work per se, but remain dependent on a learning movement on the part of the learner, which cannot be forced but can certainly be challenged and encouraged.

The deliberate promotion of such self-learning skills as well as the related research and analysis was neglected for many years. Only since the beginning of the twenty-first century has it come into its own in corresponding publications (Kaiser 2003). Such studies, however, did not change the mainstream of didactic thinking. There remained an underlying teacher-centric dominance, and efforts continued to relate more and more to the average types or to typical milieu characteristics—largely detached from the question of unique learning projects, learning foundations, and learning opportunities of the individual learner.

---

**TEXTBOX  4.5**

The enabling didactic concept, in comparison, radicalizes the relationship to the participant by designing the learning and skill development principally as a self-structured appropriation movement, attempting to resolve the presumption of a planned target group construction.

---

The question "How can you construct a typical milieu representative?" is not to be taken as a polemic, but rather meant in the sense of observation theory—after all, didactic anticipation is and will always remain the construction of an individual observer, just as Nietzsche taught us: "We still have our eye, our psychology set on it" (Nietzsche 1972, p. 51).

The systemic-constructivist forms of dealing with opposing systems, as typical in the enabling didactic, approach the worldviews and learning foundations of the participants in a different way. They develop through questioning and emerge when offered enough space, patience, and respect. This approach stems from the intransitive nature, as we find in Nietzsche's "eternally recurring thoughts."

Consequently, successful learning and competence development also comes from an "intransitive preservation of state" (Abel 1998, p. 129)—above all, from impulses, inputs, or attempted didactic controls. At the same time, the teaching functions and media in the learning process change

- Teaching moves to become professional, providing extracurricular support for processing an individual learning project on the basis of a transparent interest in competence.
- The medium itself opens a wide range of access for self-directed appropriation and, in part, replaces the teacher—an education policy polemic that is already forecasting a "teacher twilight" (cf. Türcke 2016).
- In the process, social (i.e., establishment) expectations and standards are not neglected. They are made accessible to the learner from the start in the form of competence profiles—a special type of input. By being able to access the skills required in the profile early in the process, the learners

can adapt their own portfolios, practicing their own development. The learners remain what they always have been: masters of their own learning process.

The interaction of these elements in the enabling didactic does not happen without a prerequisite—or better—a framing "teaching function." All else would be fatal in education policy and would act counter to the requirements of responsible public education. Note that this "teaching" goes far beyond the demands of instruction. Yet it limits itself far more to the creation of transparency and access support.

In this context of participant focus, the medium takes on a special importance: the medium becomes, in principle, the open door to the content. This is no longer monopolized by the teacher, but must be discovered, evaluated, processed, and appropriated by the learners. The medium loses its privilege as a decision factor but gains relevance as it must be considered a matter of course.

The living and educational worlds come to be viewed as spaces penetrated by media, which is why learning has always involved "media management" (Schiefner-Rohs 2015, p. 119) where "depth," in principle, is limited not only because media use requires technology.

A *singularity didactic* does not yet exist, but it could, and it should, if the buzzwords from Silicon Valley are to be believed. Such didactic studies would describe human self-learning—a concept that in many respects is a pleonasm, since all learning is a self-movement. This trivial fact is not essential; rather the question of what opportunities the future will provide that will account for the distinct learner traits that make each individual a singularity is important.

The learner differences require a type of training organization that can provide a variety of possible effective learning paths. This refers to the personalization of education—a goal formerly associated with differentiation (i.e., differentiated relative to the different prestructuring and needs of the learners). In this context, high expectations are assigned to the "Digital Revolution in Education" (Dräger/Müller-Eiselt 2015). Coauthors Jörg Dräger, Executive Board of Bertelsmann Foundation, and Ralph Müller-Eiselt, also from the foundation, stated:

> Today's standard education system is not the right response to the diversity of the learners; the needs of the individuals are too varied. The traditional homogeneity of our schools has long since become an illusion. . . . The promise of digitalization is an affordable education for all and customized learning for all. (ibid., pp. 37 and 40)

These authors also question, in particular, the self-image of universities and other institutions of higher learning regarding their monopoly on access to an academic education and degree program. They predict that the course of digitalization of education will leave "no stone unturned" (ibid., p. 155*ff.*), since the trend toward development of potential, prompting talent, and the personalization of education is unstoppable worldwide.

The digital learning organization is proving to be a powerful agent with regard to the implementation of the major tenets of lifelong learning, as suggested by the following alignment of the "10 Ds of a digital learning organization" (table 4.1).

**Table 4.1.   From analog to digital education**

| *10 "D" comparison of a digital with an analog learning organization* | | |
|---|---|---|
| *Learning organization* | *Analog* | *Digital* |
| **D**istribution | Frequently, learning content is only accessible to participants following an attendance or assembly model. | Relevant content is provided quickly and, in principle, worldwide (up to an open-content model). |
| **D**ifferentiation | The levels demanded and the learning speeds are determined by the average learners. | Differentiated or customized offers are possible, which follow from learning history and previous experiences. |
| **D**oors open | Often limited by membership in a certain milieu, or the acquired or neglected educational degrees as well as income and life situation. | New paths opened (e.g., acknowledgment of job-related skills and previous abilities) for exactly those target groups furthest away from educational opportunity. |
| **D**emocratization | The effective social selection for access *to* and advancement *through* education contradicts the basic premise of the equality of educational opportunity. | The effective selection mechanisms in the education system can be circumvented or compensated for by using (or being able to use) self-directed learning. |
| **D**evelopment | Personality development presupposes self-reflection and confrontation with others—both usually take place in the face-to-face context of social learning. | Social media opens the possibilities of networking (e.g., peer-to-peer groups, study groups), in which feedback is ensured on the kinds of behavior in relation to others. |
| **D**econstruction | Professionalism demands the ability to manage knowledge, its use, and further development/updates. | This sovereignty in dealing with traditional interpretations and concepts is not dependent on all learners coming together, but it can also be acquired when dealing with online texts and learning programs. |

*(Continued)*

**Table 4.1. (Continued)**

| 10 "D" comparison of a digital with an analog learning organization | | |
|---|---|---|
| *Learning organization* | *Analog* | *Digital* |
| **D**efinition certainty | Successful education and competence building are based on the certainty of terms and the depth of concepts. These are practiced in face-to-face contact as well as in demanding reading assignments. | Surfing the Internet skips the need for certainty of terms and depth of concepts; however, through deliberate confrontations in learning programs or chats, an increased awareness of these can be cultivated. |
| **D**istance | The self-separation ability and the continuous questioning of long-cherished perceptions are practiced in a seminar context. | The self-separation ability and the continuous questioning can also be strengthened through self-study or in virtual and guided phases of self-reflection. |
| **D**ialog | Real dialog requires the presence of a common learning location. | Social media also provides the possibility of rich dialog. |
| **D**egree | Public education requires a state-owned or socially responsible certification monopoly. | Digital grading and certification (e.g., peer-to-peer evaluations) of abilities is also possible. |

At its core, the didactic concept of singularity is a self-study didactic—to a certain extent, an enabling didactic *plus*. It takes the demands of an effective learning arrangement into consideration for self-learning opportunities and, in some ways, turns the didactic model of the past on its head.

Content, lesson plans, and curricula, as well as teacher activities, no longer permeate throughout all didactic logic, because "more and more avenues are available with digital teaching materials" (ibid., p. 72). Consequently, "teaching adapts to the learner, no longer the learner to the teaching" (ibid.). This is a quantum leap in didactic thinking with increasingly evident consequences for enabling learning, but also with implications that remain unforeseeable for the eligibility system of degrees and titles.

## NOTES

1. In an interview, Klaus Holzkamp said: "I am attempting to show the various contexts in which the idea that the process of learning can be planned in advance with didactic solutions such as lesson plans and teaching strategies (i.e., prepared conditions) is a fiction: nothing is left for the learner other than to learn in the manner desired. In truth, such pre-arrangements decided beyond the minds of the

learner, the resistance, the refusal, the evasions—if it ever comes to real learning at all—is oriented on 'defensive learning,' not on the penetration of the topic, a deeper understanding of the content, etc. Rather to satisfy only the teachers' need to avoid the imposition of sanctions, i.e., to demonstrate success even if faking it" (Holzkamp 1996, p. 31*ff.*).

2. This program is described in press release no. IP/06/1148, dated September 5, 2006, titled "The European Qualifications Framework: A New Way to Understand Qualifications across Europe" (www.europa.eu/rapid/press-release_IP-06-1148_de.pdf).

*Chapter 5*

# Learning Is Less Preparation and More Identity Formation

Education and learning have been understood for centuries as "equipping to cope with life's situations," as the curriculum theory still presents it to us to this day. Curriculum development requires the predictability of expected requirements—a task that can only be reliably mastered if the future stays more or less the same as the past has been.

For a long time, this has been the case, but it has changed dramatically in just the past few years: the pedagogy of preparation has become obsolete and increasingly gives way to the pedagogy of empowerment (refer to figure 5.1). This concept is dependent on making people fit to deal with new and uncertain situations. Certainty is being replaced by uncertainty in learning or in equipping learners for success in mastering new and uncertain situations.

According to all the indications from Silicon Valley, modern twenty-first-century societies will undergo an intensity of change never before experienced in the previous 20,000 years of human history. The need for a fundamental change in the pedagogic paradigm of preparation should not be overlooked. While learners still have to be prepared for the future, the greater issue is how such preparation is even possible in view of the uncertainties of the future.

Included in the discourse is the idea of "self-sharpening" qualifications or so-called reflective abilities, aimed not so much at detailed preparation for predictable change, but rather at reinforcing a person's ability to deal successfully with new requirements of any kind and at any time.

One future certainty is that people will have to prove themselves in various domains: some will pursue engineering or scientific expertise, while others will train for health care, social, or other new work. The appropriation of domain-wide knowledge and abilities, therefore, will remain an essential element of future-oriented education.

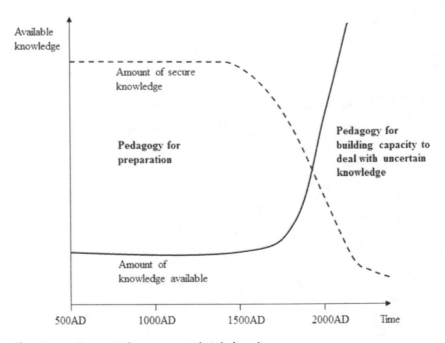

**Figure 5.1.   From certainty to uncertainty in learning**

However, we must distance ourselves from maddening levels of detail and completeness, which often lead to overloaded lesson plans, as well as training and study provisions with expertly detailed knowledge. Only with a presumptuous gesture can it be claimed—and demonstrably proven—that this is of crucial importance for the future. Such a gesture escapes the trend toward the enabling pedagogy of empowerment described earlier.

Rather, it takes the path of learning certainty, which does not allow for the development of competency when faced with uncertainty. Even employer representatives are calling for a new focus, while pointing out that modern education should include "more than specialization" (VbW 2015). Contemporary education research is struggling for concepts and strategies for effective personal development anchored in contemplative principles.

One topic of discourse is the necessity to strengthen the self-reflective view that enables people to imagine the world in unfamiliar terms and to shape it accordingly: "We experience not only our original view, but the multiple views of others, synthesizing them," wrote Artur Zajonc, director of the Center for Contemplative Mind in Northampton (Zajonc 2014, p. 27).

The pedagogy of empowerment distances itself from the mechanistic input concept, which ultimately depends on the illusion that future competence requirements can be anticipated. Empowerment is much more results-oriented. The focal point is on the outcomes while being aware that these cannot be calculated or forced. For this reason, the designs and strategies primarily look at the question of how appropriation can achieve the development of required competencies and transformation of the individual.

Diversity is the order of the day: if we cannot know for sure what actually triggers the learner's resonance and willpower to support a "transformation" (Rosa/Endres 2016) to new perspectives and expanded competencies, then it only makes sense to increase the number of possibilities and "rooms" or frames for appropriation—for example, arranged contexts. Instructional scenarios are replaced by learning environments, where learners can linger and explore alone or with guidance. They are not moved along a path to a destination, but rather are asked to find their own way.

The urge to overwrite this heading with the Buddhist expression "the journey is the destination" is strong. But this would be simplistic and imprecise. Merely wandering, exploring, or lingering is just as simplistic, although these are precisely the abilities that learners so desperately need for their own lifelong learning process. At the same time, they are moving in a thematically arranged context.

In such a context, learning opportunities are designed that will most likely confront the learner in the chosen domain currently as well as in the future. The curricular approach is not entirely dismissed in the pedagogy of uncertainty; however, it appears in the logic of controlled context, not (no longer) one of controlled input.

## REMOVING THE RESTRICTIONS ON LEARNING

Knowledge, or the access to knowledge, and the marked differences accruing from the certified possession of knowledge represent *the* key element for individual success in knowledge societies. Biographies are stories of education and knowledge. They tell of the efforts an individual has made in life to acquire an education and expertise—not only in the context of a formal, but also in an informal learning setting (on the job, in honorary office, etc.).

The decisive information, however, is not the knowledge and skills, rather the evaluations and certifications. We live in a society of titles. Only a certified training success is a biographical success—an unbroken logic. That is why European education policy is striving to assign effective informal learning, as well as lifelong learning, to the prevailing certification mechanisms that ensure advancement through education.

These efforts have contributed to a greater permeability in the sometimes columned pathways of institutionalized education. Those who possess the required skills but are unable to present an educational degree can still gain access to continuing education and positions. Nevertheless, this leaves modern societies doubly uncertain, as they must question whether such efforts actually relate to a confirmation of ability or whether they are not bringing judgmental educational standards through a back door. They do not know what skills can be coupled to what standards in their certification decisions because the knowledge base is dynamically increasing and changing.

To clarify these questions, it is necessary to have more and more distance from traditional ideas about knowledge and set out on a new path to think about knowledge differently. It is no longer sufficient to present knowledge as a compilation of complex and structured explanations that fit between two book covers. In earlier efforts to differentiate the issue of content, education theory made a difference between material and formal education—a distinction that could be helpful in preparing a new version of the concept of knowledge.

The basic idea is that the so-called material knowledge composed of subject matter requires a formal or reflective knowledge in order to be properly ordered, understood, and evaluated. Only a formal or reflective education allows the learner to become a source of knowledge. For not all knowledge is explicit knowledge, that is, written, documented, and transmittable, and also, the written word is always subject to a loss of validity.

Informal knowledge and the habit of appropriation as the way of dealing with knowledge play a major role in the resolution of new kinds of problems. Knowledge appears on one hand as a reference to a clarification and regulatory know-how, while on the other hand as an ability to successfully apply, evaluate, and expand in the process of managing new situations. The lines of separation between knowledge and competence have blurred, and knowledge, while being a necessary component of ability, has been dematerialized—a development that is not without its problems. Nobel Prize winner Robert Shiller proposes:

> People used to be defined by their knowledge. If you knew a lot, you were interesting. Today, we do not need so many interesting people because of the internet, where anyone can find the answer to any question—and indeed, very often a much better one. . . . If acquired knowledge is devalued en masse, individual identities are threatened. The whole idea of self-esteem is based on the ability to do something. Self-esteem today is devalued. (Shiller, cited in Beise/Schäfer 2016, p. 208)

Such ideas illustrate that in clarifying the question of what knowledge is and what forms are increasingly important in a modern society, long-cherished conceptions have to be examined. This applies, in particular, to the widespread notion that knowledge is a certain possession to be acquired from others—experts, teachers, authors—an idea subjected to a cynical critique by Latin American pedagogue Paolo Freire (1921–1997) and published in the 1970s (Freire 1985).

He directs attention to the questionable nature of the idea that education is a kind of investment, which lets external assets be invested in people for the promise of a return. According to him, this is a naive interpretation of what education is and could be, and he counters with the concept of a process, in which people enrich, develop, and express their inner assets. This critique of the concept of material education, where content originates from traditional subject matter and has little connection to the worldview of the learner, allowed Freire to anticipate many of the later concepts, mostly represented in adult education that are more learner focused, and to emphasize the movement to express and expand inner choices.

In this way, Freire also takes account of the always-dormant everyday abilities of his clientele, which were only lacking their own concepts and ideas. Literacy, said Freiere, always includes more than merely acquiring a skill; it is also a formation of consciousness, which places a person's own being and abilities into perspective, which rehabilitates it in a certain way, to promote enlightenment as an expansion of one's own possibilities for dealing with the world.

Similarly, learner-focused movements have been observed since the turn of the century in areas that concern the development of technical and professional skills. In these areas, there was a growing insight that expert knowledge was fundamental, although this was not enough of a basis for competent action in the various domains (i.e., special subject areas).

The "dormant" abilities, knowledge, and skills of the person are also essential to the way they behave in the work process and which explanation or factual knowledge they are actually able to relate to in a given situation. This so-called work process knowledge took on a greater significance—knowledge that is not found in textbooks, but much more through observed procedures. This refers to knowledge forms that correspond more to Type B than to Type A knowledge (table 5.1).

**Table 5.1. Removing the restrictions on learning**

| | *Knowledge as a possession→*<br>*(Type A)* | *Knowledge as a process*<br>*(Type B)* |
|---|---|---|
| Aspect | Material<br>Explicit<br>Passive | Reflection<br>Implicit<br>Active |
| Knowledge management | Knowledge management as learning and "sharing" of existing or required knowledge | Knowledge management as the empowerment to participate in shaping knowledge |

This comparative view illustrates the major limitations that knowledge is subject to in modern societies, where in many ways it degenerates to a fundamental, but nevertheless instable, developmental reference point. The dimensions of delimitation are as follows

- You have to differentiate material from reflective knowledge.
- Knowledge overall is hard to explicate; its successful use is a blend of implicit experiences and the knowledge and skills of the person.
- Knowledge is not a passive possession, but rather an active and helpful possibility (cf. Argyris 1997)—this is the competence dimension, which is often ignored in the discourse or is even deemed irreconcilable with actual knowledge.
- Knowledge is even more accessible in electronic media, which implies the linkage to the person who holds it is increasingly replaced by self-sufficient knowledge in "networks" (Neuser 2013, p. 47):

In our present society, knowledge is a grounded interplay of many fragments of knowledge, which are technically combined in the World Wide Web (www) and exist there as commonly available knowledge constituted by a process of knowledge formation as a community experience. This concept of knowledge is a new one. (ibid.)

In cognitive theory, delimiting (merely) passive knowledge to active knowledge and separating knowledge from a single individual is essential. If the outcome is to be sustainable and not merely fleeting, learning and competency development must always be about appropriation and keep the individual in mind. The person may no longer be the keeper of knowledge but may remain the keeper of competence.

Competence arises from sustained appropriation. This does not result from memorizing detailed information and an additive connection to a more or less coherent body of knowledge—aspects of knowledge the web has already adopted with amazingly reliable processes. Competence is much more about weighting and ordering details in a well-founded inner disposition structure.

Acquiring, appropriating, and using knowledge and skills continue as before to make up the core of the learning process; however, these are accompanied by constant shifts in the boundaries between the net and the learner. What happens is of more substance than the mere storage of information. A person who uses knowledge as a feature of competent action understands the coherent and structured interplay of explanations and, therefore, is able to access, classify, and evaluate scattered information.

Learners are expected to develop this competence and, in the process, gain an increasing certainty of the relevant facts while at the same time remaining open to a changing basis of knowledge. Under examination, it can be determined if and to what extent this has been successful and if the learners are able to apply their knowledge to solve problems, that is, to transpose it to *active knowledge.*

Testing is able to determine this ability only to the level of qualification. It can describe behavioral dispositions: the candidate being tested can only demonstrate whether he or she is able to describe an approach to a solution and, for example, how he or she would go about processing the tasks. The person's real competence, on the other hand, is the competence shown when demanded for real life—in serious situations.

The focus is on reflective forms of knowledge in such situations. These forms include not so much stored insights, knowledge, and explanatory relationships, but instead as seen in the ability to independently develop the current and effective knowledge supply (e.g., new technologies) or to master crises and cooperate in solving problems and to share the knowledge with others.

Since the 1980s, the discourse has included the idea of key qualifications and a clear plea to pay more attention to them in the processes of personality development and in the development of reflective forms of knowledge. In this context, reflection refers to the ability to subordinate your own opinions and actions with good reason, so as to have an unbiased perspective and to learn from mistakes. This ability can be cultivated by learning from complex tasks as illustrated in the following design process of instructional material.

## AGING OF KNOWLEDGE OR SHIFTING OF KNOWLEDGE FORMS?

The discussion is about the ever-shorter half-life of knowledge, referring to the fact that certain forms of knowledge and abilities are becoming 50 percent obsolete at ever-shorter intervals—in other words, pointless. Becoming obsolete is a development that is estimated to take twenty years in the field of academic learning, but approximately one year in the area of information technology (cf. Löffler 2001).

This insight was popularized, in particular, by mathematician and network researcher Samuel Arbesman. In his book *The Half-Life of Facts* (Arbesman 2012), he discussed the time interval required for new discoveries and evidence-based facts to replace previous scientific knowledge, either completely or in part. As a representative of the fairly young discipline called "scientometrics," he examines the exponential growth curves of knowledge development and knowledge obsolescence in various disciplines and illustrates, by means of many examples, how much time human thinking and human abilities need to acquire an understanding of recent innovations.

We can almost get the impression that knowledge is moving exponentially, while the human capacity to learn is only able to follow a linear growth function. In this context, the following chart has been published and is often cited for its impressive documentation of the half-life intervals of knowledge differentiated in particular subject areas (figure 5.2). The lesson is clear:

---

**TEXTBOX   5.1**

We cannot continue to supply our youth with "required knowledge," in learning phases sometimes lasting ten years (e.g., at universities) when that knowledge will already be 50 percent obsolete within two years. The half-life of knowledge poses a paradoxical counterpoint to the typical tendency in a modern society to prolong the time of education (in some cases, until the third decade of a lifetime). A redistribution of schooltime throughout the curriculum vitae is the logical and necessary consequence.

---

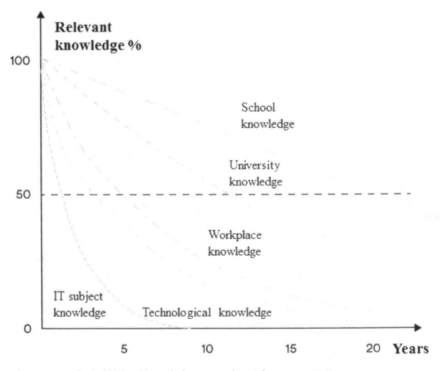

Figure 5.2.   The half-life of knowledge (see Schüppel 1996, p. 238)

The half-life argument is not without controversy. The idea that such a prognostic quantification of knowledge and skills development is even possible and acceptable is cast into doubt (cf. Klemm 2002). There is also a question as to whether the ascertained increase in knowledge actually (almost automatically) results in the obsolescence of existing knowledge or is this just a myth, as Ulrich Walter, former astronaut and professor at the University of Munich, suggests:

> It is true that the volume of scientific knowledge doubles approximately every five years. But, the additional knowledge does not necessarily question the assured knowledge, instead it extends it to boundaries that were previously not considered reachable. This often results in superordinate theories that include the old theories. . . . On closer examination, yesterday's knowledge turns out to be the solid foundation necessary to build the expanded theories of today. Not decay, but eternal truth is the hallmark of scientific knowledge and that is precisely what set it apart from the flood of non-scientific knowledge. (Walter 2013)

The media expert Christian Wolff assigns the half-life theory to the category of a "myth of the knowledge society" and questions the methods as well as the admissibility of far-reaching conclusions drawn from bibliometric findings (e.g., number of publications, citation dates). In his opinion, these are often inadequate or even suspect. For example, the reason for the observed preference for recent literature may simply be the easier access to it in the institutes and libraries (not the obsolescence of older publications), although generally "every one-time published work has a uniform chance of being read" (de Solla Price 1974, p. 92).

Wolff writes about the observable preference in recent literature: "Such attitudes may in fact lead to shorter half-lives, but there is absolutely no reference on which to base the validity of the knowledge base" (Wolff 2008, p. 17).

Let that be as it may. If the total of available knowledge increases dramatically, then logically the number of possible interpretations in the development of appropriate controls also increases. This has a fundamental effect on the notion of completeness for what is to be learned and known: doubling the supply of knowledge at ever-shorter intervals not only leads to constant updating and supplementing the effective knowledge base of skills, but it is also accompanied by the loss of half of what was previously valid.

The tendency toward obsolescence confronts not only the individual, but also the education system with fundamental issues. These concern the requirement for responsible public education to prepare learners. The question is how the education system can satisfy this requirement in the future so that learners are truly able to acquire *the* competencies that will help them to master new kinds of problems in a self-directed and professional way—as defined in the European Qualification Framework (cf. Arnold 2015, p. 47*ff.*).

Professional aptitude, without a doubt, requires access to state-of-the-art knowledge concerning the respective domains. But how can learners manage, for example, those enrolled in a multi-year degree program, when a significant portion of their subject study is already obsolete when they complete their program?

Could it be possible that the aging curve, with a varying half-life index of one to two years (for IT subjects), eleven years (for university learning), and twenty years (for school learning), represents an opposite trend? This curve reflects that the more the half-life of "relevance of knowledge" shortens, the greater is the significance of personality development and extra-professional competency, especially, in areas where exponential growth functions.

This view, in turn, inevitably leads to paradoxical considerations: in particular, educational institutions that are highly specialized (IT expertise, engineering sciences, professional knowledge) would increasingly have to develop into venues of general personality formation that prepare learners to deal with professional as well as personal changes and reinforce the strategies and skills demanded for the "struggle of lifelong learning" (Baethge/Baethge-Kinsky 2004). These institutions would increasingly distance themselves from the basic pedagogic patterns of "safe preparation" and focus instead on the practice of managing uncertainty.

Indications of the accelerating change in economic and societal relationships are not new. This already began with the industrialization of European societies in the nineteenth century and continues today to accompany us on the path to the postindustrial knowledge society.

The early analysis by David Bell is worth noting, above all his dynamic factors of development and the exponential duplication of knowledge (Bell 1975): "which will inevitably lead to the increasing inadequacy of information—in other words, we know less and less" (ibid., p. 353).

We are not so much troubled by the fact that we must constantly learn something new as by the fact that we have to cope with an ever-growing shortage of knowledge appropriate for the situation. At the same time, more uncertainty exists as the requirements increase. A survey carried out by CEDEFOP in four EU member states (Germany, Hungary, the Netherlands, and Finland) in 2011 concluded that only 16–30 percent of those surveyed were of the opinion that the level of training necessary to complete their work assignments was "the same or lower" than when they started (CEDEFOP 2012).

An overwhelming majority of the workers shared the feeling that they must come to terms with being "inadequately informed" (Bell 1975, p. 353) while concurrently trying to meet the expectations of the current markets and customers. Against the background of such assessments, the idea of "completeness" loses significance and vanishes ever more in the questions of the times. This refers to a fundamental switch in our understanding of curriculum content: while "completeness" is a container term, "timeliness" is a change term.

---

### TEXTBOX  5.2

Completeness is a category of certainty learning.

---

Schools and training institutions could be pleased by the hypothesis that learners only have to acquire the wealth of coherent domain knowledge or its categorical structures in order to secure a sufficient basis for their expertise. The trends outlined earlier question this hypothesis. In particular, what would such a basis for expertise look like when, in just a few years, 50 percent of the domain knowledge has actually become obsolete? Is it not counterproductive to guide the professional learning process onto such shaky ground?

No longer oriented on claims of completeness, the Internet has opened convenient, new forms of lifelong learning that provide timely access and focus on contemporary problem solving. But what does it mean for our own competence and our own identity, when the knowledge we possess slips through our fingers and disappears?

### SELF-COMPETENT, BUT EXHAUSTED?

The trends toward self-empowerment are not without controversy. Anthropologists and psychologists as well as brain and behavioral researchers increasingly agree that humans are a self-structured animal par excellence (cf. Damasio 2011). However, there are apparently two sides to the coin. A growing self-responsibility may also lead to an overburdening of the individual, which can interrupt the comfortable trance of a controlled glide. In this context, there is a well-known classroom joke:

> When the teacher enters the classroom with a mediator's briefcase and flip charts, a student asks with a concerned look: Professor, do we have to do again today whatever we want to do, or can we do what you want to do?

Self-competence can be rather ambivalent—a fact that until now has not been given much attention in the educational sciences. Until now, these have celebrated the breakout of the self, which without exhaustion or even a doubt can proceed down the path of individualization.

Although the self can benefit from the greater possibilities for shaping its world and escaping from the rituals of an externally controlled development strategy, this also seems to demand a lasting presence that can be tiring and exhausting. The French sociologist Alain Ehrenberg examined, in his German language book *Das erschöpfte Selbst: Depression und Gesellschaft in der Gegenwart* (Ehrenberg 2008), the psychosocial consequences of this move toward the self. He wrote about the constant anxiety of the "sovereign individual," which can lead to depression:

> The career of depression begins at the moment when the disciplinary model of behavior control which authoritatively assigns roles to the social classes and the two genders is abandoned in favor of a norm that requires each individual to take their own personal initiative: obliging them to become themselves. . . . This book shows that depression is the exact opposite of . . . and is the illness of responsibility, in which a feeling of inferiority pervades. The depressive is not at full strength, but is rather exhausted by the effort to find himself. (ibid., p. 15)

Is it so unreasonable to think this effort—especially, if it remains unsuccessful and cannot offer any counter to social exclusion other than itself—will tend to create a nostalgic return to the past (motto: "Everything was better before") or even a turn toward a populist oversimplification? What is left to the individual who has been set back, when they can only see their exclusion from the job opportunities, further education, and a better life through the glasses of self-responsibility?

It cannot be ignored that the growing use of a "new CV pattern" (Bolder et al. 2010) ultimately conveys a reversal of the assignment of responsibility, which is not only overburdening, but also unfair. The self can reflect on its situation, optimize the competence profile, and try to stay motivated; however, it is not able to accept self-responsibility for the macro trends in the job market or the changes in factory employment that determine the chances for promotion and development.

One thing is quite clear: increasing self-responsibility needs responsible public support to ensure the integrated development of the regimes and opportunities of life. If this does not meet with success, the pressures of individualization land squarely on the backs of the socially weak—with the result: "the privileged appear as such to themselves, deserving of their success and believing that excluding the failures is justified because they were unable to grasp it" (Kirchhöfer 2007, p. 32).

Such self-characterization must be combated. Democratic societies, as a matter of self-preservation, must endeavor to secure the individual opportunities of life and effectively counter the anger of being "left behind."

A framework of political concepts and strategies is required to counteract individualization and isolation. The shift to the self that is welcomed and celebrated in education threatens to slip into social desperation and anger if no limits are set on individual responsibility.

The individual can only be held accountable for his or her own initiative and motivation. When one person falls into the void, the society has failed and threatens a revolution of the excluded, as currently observed in many Western democracies. Though this exclusion is not the cause of the rising populism and post-factual irrationality, it does provide the fertile ground for it.

Specifically, the marginalization of the determined self favors not just the emergence of depression, but also the rising anger. While depression may still be considered the peak of self-made accusation leading to paralysis, the anger is directed outward. The angry person cannot be persuaded by facts, since the accused ego yearns to make the world responsible.

Simplifications, the assignment of collective responsibility (with regard to social or ethnic groups), and conspiracy theories provide enough justification for a rough orientation, while the more complex explanations are expressions of the hated world, which just does not seem capable of granting the person a chance in life. "It has long been about identity and honor," said Bernd Ulrich in *Die Zeit,* the German weekly newspaper: "which is why it is so baselessly wrong to reproach the economically disadvantaged and their moral inferiority (i.e., go low) while at the same time, behaving as if born ethically superior" (Ulrich 2016, p. 3).

That is the point! The aim of educational sciences and policy is to develop concepts and strategies that enable people to focus their self-awareness and social orientation on facts and reason and not on their emotions. This is the old concern of enlightenment and political education. However, such educational efforts can only succeed in societies capable of providing not only for individual self-responsibility, but also the social responsibility to provide lifetime opportunities of all members of the society. Political science and politics are called upon to examine and design enabling biographic contexts.

# Chapter 6

# Education Is about Seeking, Not Finding

Our idea of what education means has developed over the centuries and has sometimes been condensed into dogmatic concepts. In the beginning, it was a religious idea that God made mankind in his own image: "God created man, in the likeness of God made He him," as it appears in the first book of Moses (Genesis, Chapter 5). This was the idea that also shaped the early concepts of education.

Comenius (1592–1670) and Schleiermacher (1768–1834), in particular, took up the role as theologian and pedagogue to reinforce the idea of this likeness to God and to strengthen the idea that the true task of all education is to help bring out the divine in mankind (cf. Comenius 2008)—a role that even the secular education theories of the eighteenth, nineteenth, and twentieth centuries could not completely resolve. Nevertheless, the Enlightenment did result in a slight modification in thinking that suggested that mankind carries the fullness of its potential within and, therefore, every individual has a fundamental human right to bring this to full expression in his or her own life.

This normative claim has a bearing on educational concepts up to the present day. Immanuel Kant became the godfather in the German-speaking regions, with his definition of the Enlightenment as the liberation of mankind "from its own self-imposed immaturity." In the critical years of the 1970s, this orientation on emancipation together with equality emphasized the necessity to overcome social conditions that were often seen as restrictive and unjust. These conditions became the target because they seemed to cause or exacerbate discrimination and exclusion.

An almost euphoric desire for change spread across the entire country, but not until the 1990s was there a softening in the views about the effects of the complex interrelationships in education, especially, regarding participation and social mobility. The rise of systems theory in the social sciences saw a move toward more reasonableness in pedagogic, didactic, and education policy, and the insight gradually developed that good intentions alone ("pedagogic correctness") do not ensure a democratic education; that also needs safeguards for the appropriate *action*.

Whether and to what extent this actually succeeds in winning over the less well-educated and discouraged youth to expand their skills or to make a better start through education is—according to present knowledge—much more dependent on the initial emotional state as well as the person's past experience with self-empowerment and appreciation than on the professionalism encountered in educational and quality standards, curricula, or training regulations.

Even the critiques associated with these approaches to education are mainly inextricable with the promise of advancement and greater opportunity. They unintentionally strengthen the view that exclusively projects external demands and chances on the learner. Pushed into the background are aspects of formal education that once, in connection with Wilhelm von Humboldt, presented an alternative to material education theories.

Today, this alternative refers to reinforcing the power of the ego and the potential of the individual, supporting well-founded positions on the importance of experience, and further developing the self-image and self-directed learning skills. This requires social access to a supportive context as well as the early emotional embedding of the experiences of appreciation and self-empowerment.

Such education is less concerned with mediating specific knowledge than with promoting an inner attitude capable of questioning its own beliefs and a constant search for new, appropriate, and feasible answers. This kind of attitude formation relies on the contemplative abilities of individuals as they relate to themselves and the world around them, for example

- to fully focus your attention without the distorting whisperings of your ideas,
- to set aside your own assumptions and opinions,
- to gain insights, deeper connections with others, their needs, and situations,
- to have empathy and compassion as well as respect for the lives and views of others,
- to express trust and intimacy,
- to form a more holistic and integrated perception of causal relationships, and
- to have deeper and more active participation with others (cf. Gunnlaugson et al. 2014, p. 5).

The sustainable development of these abilities has more to do with your own emotional adjustment throughout your early development phases than with the content of later teaching plans and curricula. In later development phases, a person can still be resocialized through self-examination and guided exercises, although the original forms of dealing with oneself and the world can seldom be completely overcome.

In any case, such attitude formation demands self-reflective learning that encourages seeking and self-awareness since both are, ultimately, what subtly determine the way we manage knowledge. Those who are unable to develop the stated contemplative abilities tend to adopt an "objective" worldview that believes in technical mastery over the world and other people.

In contrast, a self-reflective/contemplative education favors the formation of an awareness, which in other concepts and behavioral patterns is seen only as an expression of the human search. Contemplative thinkers do not ask later on who may be right or wrong; they simply try to identify the patterns activated when dealing with themselves and others in the world, to improve the reciprocal connectivity. They are masters of seeking, not finding.

They are not very good at arguing over who is right. Rather, they always seek awareness of the kind Socrates demonstrated when he said, "I know that I do not know," while pointing out the real barrier to true education (the formation of beliefs and attitudes) is not ignorance, but the lack of knowledge. Only the ignorant simply hope for greater opportunity through an increase in knowledge, whereas those who know they lack knowledge have a healthy skepticism toward the hardening effect of their beliefs, which can put them in a trance and prevent them from continuing their search.

## EDUCATION: MORE THAN A WORD

Personality formation is not merely an expression, but rather a program—in fact, a rather important one. It contains the notion that a person can set out on his or her own and follow a path to become the person he or she could be (cf. Arnold 2016). This formulation may seem nebulous and ambitious and, perhaps, even more like a continuing effort than an achievement. But it nevertheless brings into focus the idea of a self-empowered education—a movement supported by the vital interest to learn "what the world looks like through different eyes" and how we can "expand our own field of vision in this way" (Spaemann 1994/1995, p. 34).

This change of perspective is at the center of a new concept of freedom, as Carolin Emcke, winner of the 2016 Peace Prize of the German Book Trade, emphasized in her acceptance address. It should be clear: just as freedom needs education, education without freedom is also unthinkable.

> We can no longer be permitted to merely claim to be a free, secular, and democratic society: we have to actually be one. Freedom is not something one owns; instead it is something one does. Secularization is not something we can finish; instead, it is an unfinished project. Democracy is not a static certainty; instead, it is a dynamic exercise in dealing with uncertainty and criticism. A free, secular and democratic society is something we must learn over and over again. By listening to each other, thinking about each other, and becoming active together in word and deed; in mutual respect for the individual uniqueness and diverse ways of belonging, and last but not least, in reciprocal admission of our weaknesses and our ability to grant forgiveness.
>   Is this difficult? Yes, absolutely. Will there be conflicts between different practices and beliefs? Yes, certainly. Will it be tricky to create an equitable balance between different religious references and the secular order? Definitely. But why indeed should it be easy? We can always start again. What is it going to take to do this? Not really so much: some strength of character, some cheerful courage and, last but not least, the willingness to change one's perspective so that more and more of us find ourselves saying: "Wow. So this is what it looks like from up here." (Emcke 2016, p. 14)

Seeing a number of different perspectives opens different possibilities for selfhood, as in our own actions in our personal and social relationships. This orientation carries both an individual dimension as well as a social one, as it also includes a requirement to shape the social framework conditions that permit and support various individual searching movements.

Education theory has always been more comprehensive than merely a rational for the selection of content that will have a forming effect as promised by the dominant social trends. The preferred content, recognizably, marks the "individual portfolio" (Lenzen 1997, p. 951) required to participate in culture and society and necessary to secure the public realm on the basis of a deep passion for the use of reason.

It was the bourgeoisie (the middle class) that decisively influenced this content and consolidated it to the dominant understanding of a general education. For a long time, the classical secondary school was the guardian of this program, which allowed the canonized cultural portfolio to become the individual portfolios.

However, the content profile was not unchallenged. The justification and the value of vocational training over a general education was repeatedly emphasized. Nevertheless, the theories of vocational education had a difficult time to escape the suspicion of serving a hidden purpose. The predominant discourse identified the classical content of the schools too strongly with the aspired personality development, as if the latter was quasi-automatically achieved through the elegance and the cultural depth of the selected subject content.

Only gradually did the discourse open to the social sciences and, in particular, to the psychological question of what is meant by personality and what context experience is needed for it to develop. This continued to hold sway almost up to the present day when further dimensions of education theory were subjected to a rational review

- "education as an individual asset,"
- "education as an individual process," and
- "education as a self-transcendence and the higher learning of the species" (ibid.).

Although these aspects of the concept of education were not totally new or unexpected; working with historical backgrounds, they were prepared as a formal education concept. Yet this preparatory work remained oddly unspecific and, ultimately, was unable to disengage from the delusion that the formal power of the individual, in contact and in confrontation with cultural content, would enable the development of an "individual portfolio" and objectify, deepen, and improve overall performance.

The details and under what conditions this transformation is to be staged to effect the formal development process remained mostly in the dark. Of course, a positive effect was expected from personal encounters and the relationship between teacher and learner, but it was hardly able to specify these aspects of the teaching process. Education remained a latent portfolio illusion. Not until the 1980s was any consideration given to the view that it is the learners themselves who select and transform the content in the learning process—autonomously and supported by the personal, social, and methodical competence they possess (or not).

What could be more obvious than the attempt to take the paradoxical step and support the learners' selection and transformation by promoting their personal, social, and methodical competence? Caring about self-learning skills is still a paradox because it proceeds from the idea that some external influence is conceivable, even with reference to the reinforcement of skills that ultimately make people stronger, which only seems possible by inner appropriation and transformation of new insights and enhanced competence (although with the aid of self-study training courses for the constantly expanding abilities) (cf. Herwig et al. 2014).

Only in recent years has the concept of "multidimensional education" (Table 6.1) gained in acceptance, replacing the one-sided standpoint of cultural and knowledge standards regarding the processes of a guided development.

**Table 6.1.   Dimensions and implicit problems with the education concept (see Lenzen 1997, p. 951*ff.*; Arnold 2013b, p. 166)**

| Dimensions of the education concept | Comments and openings for the systemic-constructivist approach |
| --- | --- |
| "Education as an individual portfolio" **Problem: Selecting the training content** | "A warehouse of education does not exist, only teaching processes for as long as there is life in the body. The selection problem of the educational institution is a fake problem, an illusion. The teacher cannot select, only the learner selects" (Lenzen 1997, p. 952). |
| "Education as an individual asset" **Problem: Perfection of thought/ undefined normative character** | The perfection of thought "is hardly compatible with the SAE concept (= Self-organization, Autopoiesis, and Emergents) because it is a regulative idea that inadvertently simplifies the education process" (ibid., p. 953). |
| "Education as individual process" **Problem: Degree of freedom granted to the individual by the education process** | "Education as self-education is a common idea that is close to autopoiesis thought . . .. Typically, . . . the education process is designed as a procedure to be carried out by the individual based on an inner regulation of the ratio of inner determinants, freedom, and external determinants as an object of action" (ibid., p. 954). |
| "Education as self-transcendence and the higher learning of the species" **Problem: The paradoxical structure of self-mastery** | "In the self-realization movement, the person certainly observes himself to repeatedly determine: it is still not enough. This dynamic trend toward self-exhaustion logically functions only with the aid of some external quantity, a regulative idea that not only resides in the person as a kind of blueprint, but also one that the person must consciously acknowledge when viewing others" (ibid., p. 955). |

"Ideally reconstructed, an understanding of education consists of the following brief aspects:
- Education is a multiple paradox.
- Education is both a process and the result of a process.
- Education as a process is both complete (mature) and incomplete (self-mastery).
- Education as a process is both goal-oriented (perfection) and without a goal (freedom)" (ibid., p. 956).

As stated in the 2015 review "Education: More Than Specialization" by the Bavarian Industry Association (German: *Vereinigung der Bayerischen Wirtschaft*), this concept, rather, focuses on

the empirical conditions for the development of personality in the sense of identity, moral and political competence, and inter-cultural skills as well as a musical and aesthetic education. A multidimensional education begins to develop the proposals that draw attention to aspects so often held subordinate. Because any attention to these aspects was mostly kept in the background since the 1970s, there has been far too little empirical knowledge developed about the processes of personality development, as is the case in the teaching-learning processes that lead to knowledge and skills development. (VbW 2015, p. 10)

Although we may ask how personality formation can be separated from the teaching-learning processes and whether "competence" does not actually mean a *personal* appropriation of the capacity for action, this assessment clearly highlights the gradual aversion to the decades-old one-dimensional education concept, which assumed to know the—right—knowledge for competence development and was blind to the universally observable weakness of the overriding ideas of educational content and the schooling concept.

The multidimensional view of education, at the same time, took a different-view of the learner. Specifically, moving away from the perspective of the need to compare students against normative measures, or typifying them by classifying them in terms of having a preference toward a certain learning style, toward seeing education as a process that is highly unique and individual to every learner.

## FROM EDUCATION TO SINGULARITY

Typologies are popular in learning and education research. They condense typical behavior habits into patterns of dealing with the self, with others, and with content as identified by studies or educational practice. A belief that learning styles exist and that teachers can classify learners by their preference toward a certain learning style. Seldom are we aware of the constructive force at work here: we see the learning styles that we know or because they are suggested by research and we have come to expect certain behaviors from a social group.

In this way, we readily assume that a person prefers to learn visually or through images, while it may be easier for another person to advance with structured and conceptual or deductive reasoning in his or her learning process. Yet what have these specific people done to us that we look at them through such preconceived notions? Are we really seeing the true case at hand, or are we blocking the learners from appearing to us in their singularity?

### A difference revolution

The greatest danger of typologies is that they tend to dissolve the *singular* into an average. This may be helpful in giving teachers a professional orientation to follow, sparing them from detours, and equipping them with suitable forms of action. But where do these paths lead? Do they always lead to the desired goal, or are they more likely to be detours and dead ends? Thought to be evidence-based, because we can justify our process on research results and statistical truths, we may actually be overlooking the coarseness of these truths.

In his book *The Granular Society*, Christoph Kucklick criticizes the average, which he describes as the "measure of modern times" (Kucklick 2015, p. 9): "Every person is unique, a singularity. . . . If we know the details well enough, the group average is irrelevant" (ibid., pp. 38 and 48).

Although this call for adequate observation and action regarding singularity is now experiencing the wind at its back from individual concepts of education theory and practice, it is also turning the idea of professionalism almost back to zero: namely, professionalism was understood as evidence-based action and valued evidence over generalization and the universal.

Those who learn to consider expertise and evidence in their responses act on the law of statistically average probabilities that sacrifices the special to describe the individual in the context of the typical. Expertise is therefore a response to the average. In specific cases, this is not what the actual case is. Professionalism risks losing contact to the individual case. Professional expertise, generally, remains related to the other person but overlooks—not infrequently, surprisingly,—their uniqueness.

How could professionalism think about supporting the search movements differently, guided and enabled in another way? Could the "difference revolution," as suggested by Christoph Kucklick, enable another perspective of an individual and the society?

> The new resolution reveals previously hidden differences, even between us as human beings. We are radically insular, singularized—and these differences are further socially accentuated and exploited. We are experiencing a crisis of equality that is already changing our workplace and our democracy. (ibid., p. 11)

This "crisis of equality" strikes at the heart of the educational concept, which since the Enlightenment has owed to all people—whatever their origin—an effort to support equal opportunity and provide for their inner growth and chances in life. The difference was clearly the starting point. However, this point has been more and more submerged by the force of scientific generalization.

The focus remained on the ideal-type self, which consigned the individual increasingly to the background. But the factual is expressed not only by generalized statements, but also by the singularity. Numerous studies of evidence-based professional actions prove too coarsely granulated for today's needs, whereas the finer-grained insights allow us in many ways to start from scratch: we realize that statistical truths only let us recognize an average, not the special that we have liberated through professional "self-inclusive reflection" (Varela et al. 1992).

> We may be largely free from the trance of our own beliefs, but we quickly succumb to prefabricated interpretations from literature and science, inserted between our open observations and the singularity of the other person. (Arnold 2016, p. 212)

Especially, in light of the talk about a post-factual society, there are two reasons why it is of primary importance to always reconfirm the meaning of evidence-based actions, especially, in the teaching process: on one hand, not everything that seems to be the case is actually factual. On the other hand, we have no choice but to seek the validity of our understanding in shaping our worldview and society. This is not achieved merely with averages, but it also requires a calculation for the singularity.

An essential requirement for this is an attitude that allows you to deal not only with your own cognitive-emotional cohesion in different—new—ways, but also with those of the other person. This means a rethinking of effect and effectiveness. By mercilessly revealing the unintended and sometimes even counterproductive developments of well-minded interventions, our professional actions can begin to depart more and more from the linear-mechanical concepts with their if-then promises.

At this point, situational-procedural approaches meet with opposing systems and respect their singularity. Professional acknowledgment of this singularity takes the form of purposeful observation and support, not goal-focused intervention. This professional movement does not first follow the rough-grained "objective knowledge" of what is given and possible, but instead, a professional ability to "calculate a reality," as this professional approach is referred to by Fritz B. Simon:

> People are non-trivial machines. This is not only true for their psyche, which changes over the course of their life (dependent on the past), but also for their body. This retains many structural characteristics for a lifetime, but it is also capable of learning. The brain changes its neuronal connections over the course of the learning history of the individual, and the immune system develops defense mechanisms against the pathogens that come into contact. All these internal changes imply that the reactions of the organism, which always operates in the here and now, remain unpredictable as far as the future is concerned. Whether it develops an illness or not, is—at least as far as most (i.e., not all) diseases are concerned—not determined by straight-line causality. The same is true for the behaviors exhibited by an individual. They are also unpredictable. Thankfully, only a few people actually live out their non-triviality and act as unpredictably as they could. (Simon 2006, p. 40)

**TEXTBOX   6.1**

The ability to "calculate" or—in other words—to "understand" our behavior and that of the other person on the basis of specific preconditions and features is essential for the effective support for searching movements (Arnold 2016, p. 226).

It is not some typology or factual provision that determines what individuals can do or express through their behavior; instead, it is their inner possibilities. These are what provide the good reasons for the behavior. In terms of supporting the search movements of another, it is not about what our "vision is, but rather what it does" (Senge et al. 2011, p. 365). To be effective, such professional support requires an awareness of the "energy and commitment" (ibid., p. 367*ff.*) of the other person's system: a guide for observing the "calculation" of their specific inner reality, what it could be, and, therefore, keeping what it promises—free from assumptions about typology or causality (cf. de Shazer 2006, p. 98).

*Chapter 7*

# Self-Study Skills Are the Key to Change

The discourse on self-learning abilities marks the turning point from an input-oriented to output-oriented education concept. In the late 1990s, this turn began to dominate the thinking about education and training as well as teaching and learning. The educational discourse turned toward greater rationality, becoming increasingly distant from traditional claims of effectiveness. There was also a sharper focus on the importance of informal learning over the course of the lifetime. The essential insights credited for this turn toward rationality are as follows

- The vast proportion of the abilities needed by an adult to successfully manage his or her jobs and life are acquired external to and independent of the institutionalized teaching processes (cf. Livingston 2006).
- Often overlooked and underestimated is the importance of learning in the family, in an honorary office, in political engagement, as well as in the workplace, and even through the Internet and the smartphone.
- Life's early experiences in dealing with the self and the environment have proven to be lasting and formative such as our experienced excitement, activation, relationships, encouragement, and our (mostly experimental) search movements and attempts at problem solving. The upper- and middle-class social milieus provide a more effective arrangement for learning development than the lower social milieus. The educational disadvantage, intolerable in a democratic society, is rooted in the differentiation of social milieus with inequities in motivational surroundings and encouragement styles as well as different educational concepts and opportunities.
- As a rule, younger generations acquire sustainable competencies when they are exposed to an appreciative and trusting atmosphere in which they are able to deal with concerns and issues that have meaning for them. Such

contexts provide space for their initial motivation, in contrast to contexts experienced as not meaningful, which refers to external motivation (through teachers) where no lasting effect is achieved. Consequently, it may be stated:

Only in person-to-person relationships, that is, when a child feels acknowledged and appreciated as an individual by another person, is it possible to open up and accept the knowledge and skills, the ideas and experience of the other person. Relationships in which a child—or later, an adult—is treated as an object and made into an object for the evaluations, expectations, intentions, and interests of others hinder this acquisition and force unfavorable learning experiences. Children primarily learn under such conditions to protect themselves from such people and their intentions, either by making that person an object for their own alternatives or by learning to view themselves as an object and behaving as one. (Hüther 2016, p. 59)

Self-learning skills are established early in life and are quickly internalized as mental patterns and routines. Much evidence indicates that preconditioning can be mitigated through compensatory efforts by schools and educational policy, but never completely overcome. At the same time, substantial evidence shows reflective learning experiences and training methods in later phases of life are not without effect.

Self-study students profit from the chance to consider their own competence in dealing with themselves and in taking a critical view of the learning requirements. They also benefit from the chance to understand the possibilities and limitations of their own routines and to practice effective forms of discussion, appropriation, and cooperation in the learning process. The basis of such self-learning practices are concepts that can be listed together in a *competence tableau* (figure 7.1).

The tableau marks the inner paths to action—appropriate actions through self-initiative and self-direction—in short, sustainable actions for problem solving. Of course, life is not just a series of "problems," but then, this term does not relate only to problematic situations; instead, it is about penetrating, explaining, and working out the new complex relationships that confront us in our professional and private lives.

- *Spiritual competence*, which is increasingly forgotten in our turn toward realism and is suppressed into the realm of esotericism, is the true core of all personality development. The "inner growth" transforms the learners' values and ethical standards as well as their possible actions and reveals what special significance the learners choose to express with their lives. Spiritual competence is the ability to perceive yourself and the world in terms of the "big questions" and to act accordingly (cf. Astin et al. 2011).

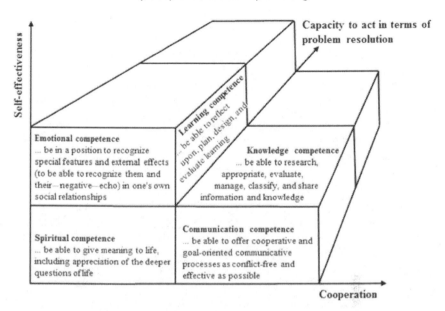

Figure 7.1. Tableau of self-learning abilities

- *Emotional competence* refers to the ability to gain a deeper understanding of yourself. The self-expression of emotions reveals how we have been taught to survive in the world before we have time to interpret and assign a meaning to it. Self-reflective emotional action requires a deeper under-standing of the fact that we are unable to see others as they are, but only as we have learned to see and feel. We must question what this says about ourselves and become aware that others are not responsible for how we (are able to) experience them. The emotionally competent person is able to avoid imposing their own expectations and attitudes onto others and instead can continuously renew the perception of the other person.
- *Communication competence* describes the ability to act purposefully and effectively in cooperative and communicative processes as free as possible from conflict. As a rule, such abilities are not learned through experience, but rather require a distanced view of the essence of the communication, as well as an understanding of the various dimensions of the act of com-municating. The further development and optimization of communicative behavior also requires practice in how to evaluate feedback in the proper context. Communicative competence develops through self-distancing, introspection and self-examination, and experience, not through a superfi-cial mechanical application of a certain set of rules.
- *Learning competence* is more like a technical skill. It includes autodidac-tic methods of preparation and systematic appropriation of knowledge and

abilities. Learning and memory techniques belong in this bundle of skills just as knowing about the different strategies for gradually developing and practicing something new. Many guidebooks and training programs for self-learning in recent years have brought this ability back into focus and point out the individual steps along the path to reach learning competence—according to the motto "step by step to competent self-learning." People who have developed their learning ability are more and more able to independently plan their own learning process. They understand the idea of ownership in the teaching-learning approaches and know their own learning belongs to them and is not to be left to others to manage and shape. The learner's ownership deprives the "'input' pedagogy" of its basis and makes it quite evident that: "Teaching cannot be saved!" (cf. Arnold 2013c).

• *Knowledge competence* ultimately includes research and evaluation skills (review and assessment), as well as the ability to manage, classify, and share knowledge and information. Those who have this competence navigate safely in a self-learning mode through the flood of information and ever-changing level of knowledge (especially, in their own domains). Knowledge competence may be considered the key competence of a modern information society in light of the extreme decrease in the half-life of knowledge (cf. Arbesman 2012).

## A RATIONAL LOOK AT COMPETENCE

The competence approach is not merely based on the thematic requirements of a subject domain. Rather, it is characterized by a different—one could almost say, an opposite—access to the processes of profiling "individual assets" (sc. abilities) and "self-transcendence," as suggested by Dieter Lenzen (1997).

More attention is given to the actual forms of expressing appropriation and competence development, without interpreting them as the primary result of experienced didactic staging, intervention, and mediation efforts—"subsystems" of systems theory. Instead of the one-dimensional concept of transferability, the competence approach takes into account the fact that it is

> the student, not the teacher, who selects. . . . Typically, . . . the education process is designed as a procedure to be carried out by the individual as an object of action on the basis of an internally regulated ratio of inner determinants, freedom, and external determinants. (ibid., pp. 952 and 954)

Access to this issue in education is associated with a fundamental rationality. It focuses on the effectiveness of learning, not the well-minded purpose. It is linked to the possible outcomes of the entitlement system and the system of assigning social status. Such a sober assessment poses an inherent explosive power.

The mechanisms for accessing higher education, professions, and positions benefit from an educational concept that contains content that differs from other mechanisms, such as vocational training or—more recently—retraining. This differentiation can hardly conceal its social functional effect: the differentiation of content serves the differentiation of society. Consequently, it works with the selection of privileged content and promises results that are rarely evidence-based, but rather—asserted—as ideological and legitimate.

As the heated debate in this conflicting situation shows, the question of whether education can truly be defined in the sense of a competence profile can hardly be discussed in an unbiased way. The current notion of education contains an inherent ambivalence, suggesting both a claim to realizing the infinite potential of self-empowerment as well as to the exclusionary aspects created by a point of view dominated by self-interest. The lack of an informed explanation of this ambivalence based on educational history implies that functions are still not openly defined, reviewed, or decided.

It is important to discover the links to the interests of the past and superimpose them on the present to see if they can be rationally continued or better left behind. A democratic society, ultimately, cannot accept a content structure in its education systems and the distribution of opportunities that are indebted to the interests of particular social strata.

This is what happened rather effectively when special interests managed to insert socially binding and long-term propositions into the lesson plans and curricula, in addition to regulations for educational advancement, which as a result have since been marginalized and permanently devalued, particularly when considering the current popularity of learning in the workplace and lifelong learning.

What is needed is a thorough redefinition of *the skills* that we can rightly say have a personality development dimension. Certainly, expertise has a major role to play. We expect competent people to appropriately manage the issues and problems of the chosen domains in which they see their future. Those who have this ability have acquired more than skills and knowledge. They have developed an ability to shape solutions that they can practice, test, and justifiably rely on. This statement illustrates the need, in addition to all expertise, for individual development and positioning as a self-organizing talent—an ability that modern educational institutions have a fundamental duty to initiate and promote.

Outcome-oriented interpretations of education issues have precedents. These can be found in the pedagogic debates of the 1980s (cf. Brater 1988). The concept of professional competence that included more than just specialist knowledge has already been profiled. There was talk of core training and the question of what methods and social skills the workers in a modern business needed to have in order to be able to deal in a self-directed manner with the constantly changing requirements in the workplace.

Even then, critics were quick to say that this acceptance of vocational education concepts was only the recognition of another subtle form of adaptation of the individual to the operational necessities. The promise of self-organization did not go far enough for them, as essential structural issues remained beyond the control of those affected.

The question had been placed in the room but was really only sporadically taken up for meaningful discussion: How much self-structuring can the host organization tolerate (cf. Arnold 2005)? Can the flexibility afforded the labor force imposed by market logic really go so far as to enable them to have a greater say in shaping the workplace and shared decision making?

These were fundamental questions—and they were accordingly judged in general terms. The fundamental debate had difficulty dealing with the simultaneous occurrence of various speed changes in business circumstances, and it often had problems finding suitable interpretations for the—initial, yet always avant-gardistic—attempts to reconcile all under one roof

- to safeguard and further develop the given organizational conditions, while at the same time
- increasing employee autonomy.

A person's ability to independently plan solutions to problems, carry out the solutions, and evaluate his or her success (as the description in the official training regulation has read since 1987) must be developed and supported in order to keep pace with the demands of the modern flexible production processes.

Many companies were forced to open up to pedagogic concepts without ever questioning their organizational structures. Still, even at that time, many of the players were aware that the abilities that characterize such competence are "comprehensive" and, in the interests of the company, could not be limited by a naive strategy. In other words:

---

### TEXTBOX   7.1

The human resource department is able to develop employees who are truly able to self-organize and accept responsibility only if, at the same time, the individuals are given a chance to voice their criticism.

---

Over time, the opening trend has been acknowledged in the matter of organizational structure. New forms of cooperation are discussed openly, and books such as *Reinventing Organizations* (Laloux 2015) or *Surviving in Diversity* (Ger. *Überleben in der Gleichzeitigkeit*) (Ehmer et al. 2016) are read and discussed by executives. Tiptoeing around the question posed in the latter book, they ask what it means when

> management, consulting, and research are required to develop practical organizational forms that not only satisfy their functional and economic missions, but are also, in recognition of their social responsibility, "people oriented."
> We need a new type of organization. A type that incorporates the contingency, i.e., the possibility, that it could be entirely different. (ibid., p. 33)

This brings the focus of change at the level of the working organizations to the concepts of action-oriented, effective competence learning that were first proposed in the 1980s. It shows that progressive companies have understood that the ability to properly shape unknown situations requires competencies that come very close to demanding autonomy in education.

Learners cannot become at least "a little bit" self-competent, unless they are allowed to use the associated skills of reflection and critique their own situation—an effect that cannot be ordered but is rather the result of expanded training concepts (key qualifications, competence training, etc.). Shaping the future requires freedom of action. The traditional corporate hierarchies and respective claims of validity have been challenged and, in a new sense, must be relegitimized.

## ONCE UPON A TIME: THE IRRECONCILABLE DIFFERENCE BETWEEN GENERAL AND VOCATIONAL EDUCATION

These developments have shaken the previous lines of argumentation in pedagogics. Until the turn of the century, perspectives were constituted by an irreconcilable contradiction between educational benefits and economic benefits. Critical educational theorists never tired of subordinating a subtly one-sided interest focus on the newer competence approaches, without noticing that they were repeating old concepts of neo-humanism: What is (can be) also useful for external purposes? Not the strengthening of the learner's self-empowerment! To this day, this is the guiding thought—powerful, yet unproven—of these skeptics.

In the final analysis, they were stuck with an educational mentality that has long since turned a blind eye to the obvious and has solidified into a fundamental skepticism. This skepticism could hardly admit that it was just pedagogic concepts that focused on the individual's ability to develop their competencies that resulted in economic benefit. These were the concepts that oriented on enabling self-structured problem solving, by supporting learners—initially unintentionally, yet unavoidably—to reflect more on the purpose of their action, to request and examine the reasons, as well as to question and evaluate joint activities.

An unbiased assessment cannot fail to reveal: currently, the most convincing attempts to *enable self-empowered individuals to make self-distancing a reality in the workplace* are to be found in vocational education, *not necessarily in the practice of pedagogics.* This assessment articulates a leap into the future of corporate training efforts, at least, as we hear from its protagonists.

In the light of the modernity advantage, it is a short theoretical leap to consider the idea that effective support of the self-organizing and problem-solving abilities will also strengthen the competencies of the learner, which are of more fundamental importance for the autonomous shaping of life than many of the declamatory claims, such as education through science or the assurances of recognized content in an education canon.

It is also appropriate to finally question the basic ideology stemming from a tradition of (requisite) pure education and to inquire about the individual competencies to be developed for self-directed, practical living. Avoid subjecting the advanced specification of the learning environment (e.g., your company) or the training methods to a general suspicion and dismissing these as a secondary importance for effective education, as is frequently the case in the current debate.

The in-depth clarification of this thesis would well-serve today's educational research, but this is often still largely ignored. What comes to mind are the initiatives in vocational education and the EU education policy to introduce the notion of competence as a more neutral and transparent category. Although many reasons exist for doing so, only a few need be listed here

- The *learner focus of the competency approach* is often perceived as particularly appropriate, since competences describe an individual faculty, which is newly produced by and anchored in each individual subject as a lasting ability. A learner-focused access is effective for individualization, while predeveloped lesson plans and curricula are created without any regard for the learner personality, and educational success is attributed linearly to the subject content and not to successful appropriation by the learner. The course offer-oriented approach hardly makes any attempt to let content be self-developed by the learner.
- The *competence approach* is different: It directs attention to the whole person—the learner's background and informal learning biography—whereas

the admission and certification regulations of the educational institutions perhaps still rely on the time spent in formal contexts and "recognized" educational qualifications acquired there. This is an unnecessarily narrow view, especially as there are many indications that people acquire the competences that support their self-organization mostly outside and independently of educational institutions. An expanded view does not go hand in hand with a rejection of the purpose of institutionalized education, but it looks beyond its present range and seeks ways to place greater credit on the importance of informal learning, especially in educational institutions. The key questions in this context are as follows: How should the institutions change in order to open themselves to the self-directed nature and informality of basic competency development? Can institutional offers be made to compensate for the disadvantages in the informal?

- Fundamental to the competence approaches of recent years is the concept of *self-organization*. In contrast to the traditional concepts, this interprets what actually happens in the learning process differently. Education and learning are rather defined as a search and discovery movement by the learner and are viewed less unilaterally as a result of various types of third-party controls. Certainly, the learners find themselves in the context of existing reality, didactically prepared and shaped, but their brains and feelings "decide" for themselves what content in this environment resonates with them and what does not. Education is self-structured, and the support of appropriating movements can only succeed if it succeeds in addressing learners—and, on their terms. Professional learning support becomes a twin search movement: it searches for suitable forms to detect, observe, and support the search movements of the learners without denying their self-organization.

- This line of argumentation conveys a new understanding of education and learning. Nothing is thrown overboard, although the proponents of competence-oriented training are sometimes in danger of "throwing the baby out with the bathwater." Then they resort to the use of exclusionary terms of demarcation, hindering the chance to connect the new to the old so as to usher in the transformation. The core principle is to develop the ability to master new kinds of problems in an appropriate and courageous as well as cooperative manner. John Erpenbeck and Lutz von Rosenstiel write in their *Manual for Measuring Competence*:

Competence is the self-structured disposition for reflective and objective actions. . . . Competence arises in the development process of more complex, adaptive systems—specifically human beings—as a general, self-structured disposition to reflect on creative problem solving, with regard for general classes of complex, selective meaning situations. (Erpenbeck/von Rosenstiel 2007, p. xi)

This definition holds that competence is an analytical category, not so much a programmatic concept. This is evident first in the competence (i.e., the ability) to handle situations and problems appropriately in a solution-oriented manner as well as in a cooperative exchange.

Competency is the expression of a person's abilities. The critics of the term "competence" like to point out that the development of competencies is not restricted to the acquisition of some silly and superficial—even repetitive—skills. Expectations of analytical or planning skills can be described as competencies. The same applies to study programs: whether and to what extent students are actually able to

- understand complex argumentation,
- discover the validity of their assumptions,
- articulate well-founded doubts, and
- use them in a balanced formulation of an independent position.

These features can all be described in competence profiles, which are then observable. Such precise descriptions of outcomes, furthermore, provide more accurate information about the attitudes and level of self-education of an individual. The competencies to be specified actually describe abilities that articulate themselves in the same dimensions on which long-term competence development also depends. These competence dimensions are as follows

- *Self-directed*: Competent actions are basically always reflected in our planning, initiatives, and process design. Advanced competence is not limited to repetition of basics or circumstances but aims at their use in dealing with specific tasks.
- *Productive*: Competent action leads to results, that is, more complex processing and designs. Whether and to what extent a person is able to master a task or actually solve a problem is seen in the end product, that is, what is achieved in the end.
- *Active*: Competent action is proactive, not simply reactive; it challenges the actor to develop and to justify their own solutions. Self-initiative that seeks ways and leaves traces, not a "wait and see what happens" approach, is fundamental to competent action.
- *Situational*: Competent action is reflected in the appropriate and proper handling of—new and unexpected—problem situations. There are also some situations that are repetitive when the ability to suspend them is part of being prepared. At the same time, the shaping of unexpected situations is a dimension that requires personality development outside of the comfort zone.

- *Social:* Socially competent action is cooperative or networked action; it recognizes the potential of others and is characterized by a division of labor and teamwork. Preparing for social participation is one of the most important dimensions in successful competence development. Progress and even innovation is no longer achieved by lone rangers; instead, it requires the ability to move naturally in relationships to protect, shape, and use them— supported by shared goals and spirit, without hypersensitivity and personal exclusion.

*Chapter 8*

# A New Understanding of Learning and How to Promote It

A multidimensional concept that sees education not as knowledge but rather as a personal asset no longer relies on the educational impact of content as we have so long assumed and come to expect. Rather, it endeavors to differentiate the subjective foundations of a consistent and self-structured handling of life's special content. A modern education theory can no longer shut itself off from the obvious fact that people can know a lot and still be unable to do anything.

If special subject content is able to establish any lasting basic abilities, then these are almost always the result of a problem-solving experience. From what we know today, people do not only follow—and often not even primarily—the better argument or the richer explanation, but what they themselves have experienced as helpful and useful. The strengthening of one's own ability to develop, transform, and evaluate knowledge is probably the only way to acquire sustainable competence.

Multidimensional educational concepts require us to have more complex access to curricular and teaching decisions. These can no longer be dealt with on the basis of the question, "What should learners learn?" Rather, they require embedding the subject content into the self-learning curriculum. If we give up on the hope that learners will somehow over time come to understand how they can most effectively realize their appropriation and transformation, what drives them to optimize their expertise, and what is slowing them down or paralyzing them, then education policy and teaching must turn to theoretically grounded and embedded strategies for shaping the teaching-learning process.

This implies the elaboration of deeper insights connected to experience, to be developed and used to replace the mediation of the new. The creation of content can no longer be automatic and considered "prime," that is, of primary importance, in didactic decisions. Instead, it is the methods used to shape the sphere of experience that open access and allow competency to develop or, in contrast, to waste away.

Specifically, this means: the focus of content must be supplemented or even superseded by a consideration of the learning process as well as the outcome. The self-development opportunities of the learner are seen as the real pivot point for long-term competence development. Education is viewed to be that which it has always been: *a development of the subjective assets of the individual.*

Teaching, in turn, becomes the enablement of search and appropriation movements, which create the desired effects through varied and inspiring didactic content design in addition to attentive learner support. All this is by no means arbitrary. It is "regulated" in a modern society in the form of standards or competence profiles, and not open to discussion.

Nonetheless, the path to fulfilling these requirements is different: it is reserved for the learners' appropriation movement and can only be paved by the learners themselves to reach the expected level of competency—or not. Insisting, intervening, or even forcing of this movement will not guarantee a sustained appropriation. And, what is even more serious is that it would deny the logic of education, which is always an inside-out movement.

Forcing an adaptation may lead to a desired behavior in the short term, but not to the deep anchoring of a subjective asset by the individual. It would only quickly fade and put the person into a restrictive corset of competence, paralyzing, and making movement impossible. Self-ability cannot be developed by disciplining. In such an environment, individuals lose the sense of their abilities, frequently, even the belief in their own ability to learn. Disciplinary appeals have been discredited, especially, in companies that depend on the learning abilities and self-competencies of their employees.

This shifting perspective has a great impact for didactic and cognitive research. Previously, this was restricted to didactic analysis (of content) and relied on the professionalism of the teachers for the selection, justification, and preparation of subject content as the all-important success factors. Today, this input orientation has been clearly called into question. It no longer corresponds to what we know today about the inner logic of appropriation.

Specifically, learning does not work from the outside in, but rather from the inside out: even the most skillful teaching of content remains ineffective over the long and medium terms, if it fails to address the learners as the administrators of their own learning ability.

The input orientation must be replaced by an *outcome orientation.* The main focus must be on a methodical analysis (the opportunity for self-development). This complements the didactic analysis and even replaces it in many ways. The primary focus on the question "What should learners learn?" is mitigated somewhat by the integration of the questions: "How should learners learn?" and "What should the outcome of effective education be?" While input-oriented ideas have their basis in content, an outcome-oriented rationale begins by questioning the desired learning outcome.

This approach assumes that those responsible are able to clearly define the expected outcome of a training session or a course of study. To this end, so-called competence profiles are of increasing importance. These profiles are where you find a list of the competencies defined to a mid level of abstraction, that is, a full and clear description of the purpose of the journey the learner is about to take. At the same time, the profiles list the skills and abilities tied to certification.

Competence profiles take the place of the lesson plans, training objectives, or module manuals. These are generally always restricted to listing areas of content, without providing any solid justification relative to the context of the desired competency. Teachers are often not in a position to convincingly justify the relevance of subject content. Many times, we hear only the traditional argument that you must know this or that in order to become, for example, a real engineer, doctor, or mechatronics specialist.

To be perfectly clear, companies need skilled employees, and the question of the necessary expertise is of central importance. However, the mere access to knowledge is not enough and favors a casual, "just get it done" mentality in the schools and educational institutions, while leaving it to the learners themselves to develop the special knowledge into a real asset. Such a transformation is not supported, or may even be hindered, if defensive forms of teaching predominate and adoption is pushed, rather than practicing appropriation. An effective outcome orientation demands more

- First, it requires teachers to learn to think differently about learning and to reflect in detail in order to challenge and overcome their deep-rooted assumptions. If they do not really understand that teaching is contrary to the learner's learning and appropriation logic and may even contribute to blocking it, then there will be little hope of a more sustainable design of learner competence development.
- The viable professionalization of teaching must focus on the observable mechanisms of transformation and the practice and consolidation of skills. This must always follow the learner's already established and proven forms of dealing with the world. The educational effect can only bear fruit when commensurate within these movements, not by ignoring them. It is essential to design learning environments in which learners can move and develop according to their own biographies.

# PEOPLE CAN KNOW A LOT AND STILL BE UNABLE TO DO ANYTHING

Not much real thought is usually given to education, but there is plenty of debate about it. Nevertheless, rationality has been spreading throughout the discussions for several years. The question of what modern societies can expect from their younger as well as their adult members has increasingly focused on the concept of competence. This term seems less mired in tradition than the concept of education, which facilitates the debate in Europe.

Other countries are not aware of either this concept of education or the associated education theories. That is why notable thinkers turned to the early use of different descriptors. For example, the German educationalist Wolfgang Klafki (1927–2016), who began long before the turn to competence to search for less traditional or regional descriptions. Klafki spoke of the need to learn how to overcome "epochal" issues. He saw in education a capacity to solve historically problematic situations—a description that already sounded a lot like today's competence approach (cf. Klafki 1993).

What qualifications and competencies will be required in the future? Although discussions are ongoing in all European countries and other countries worldwide, they are less frequently about "education" as it is understood in Germany with its very special historical roots, standards, and points of emphasis. It is not the intent, nor is it within the scope of this book to "dispose" of this point. Rather, this is an attempt to deconstruct the traditional views, examining them critically in terms of their current and future suitability.

The competence concept is devoted to a more rational discussion of the required knowledge skills and issues facing modern societies, but in so doing, it opens many more issues, which were thought for so long to be settled. This refers, in particular, to the access rules that have been defined in modern societies as a matter of course as being essential for educational success: *You can only occupy a certain position if you have completed the appropriate training courses and successfully passed the corresponding examinations.*

This certification mechanism is called into question when the importance of what courses have been attended is replaced with the primary issue of what true skills has the person learned through the academic and vocational as well as private biographies. Great advantages can accrue for an individual and the society from such open approaches, but there are also disadvantages.

These need to be thoroughly examined and discussed before giving up on the established mechanisms that, while obviously based on delusions, are nevertheless a basis of certainty for biographic planning. In the end, we do not want to be increasingly (mis)led by the force of rational insights that exhaust the modern learner (cf. Ehrenberg 2008).

Specifically, the idea is that it is perfectly appropriate to allow access to the official certifications to more than just those who stick to the prescribed path and demonstrate the standard length of stay in the educational institutions. After all, people can also acquire the competencies in other—informal—ways than we may be accustomed to seeing only in graduates of formal education.

The certification, ultimately, cannot be withheld with formal arguments. However, a prerequisite for any recognition of informally acquired competences is that the educational institutions have clearly defined what skills their graduates should actually have. This implies that they must base their work on competence profiles rather than content catalogs—a procedure that is rarely encountered today.

### *Example:*

*In professional education, you will find more and more people have advanced into positions that were, in the past, usually only open to qualified college graduates. For example, the case of in-company trainees, who after completing their occupational training (as per the German Instructor Aptitude Ordinance (Ausbildereignungsverordnung, AEVO)) become coordinators and designers of cooperative programs in a dual study program or are successful today as school guidance counselors even though they would never have had the chance to be hired as a vocational school teacher. A rational examination of their pedagogic knowledge is not available to them, although this would most likely allow them entry into an advanced course of study. Perhaps, such an examination would even reveal abilities that college graduates do not have, even though their qualifications are usually more comprehensive.*

---

**TEXTBOX 8.1**

A hot topic in the European education policy debate is how to overcome the paradox that those with formal training are often assigned to do more than they can, while the informally trained can sometimes do more than "should" be able to do.

---

The idea is to remove the artificial barriers between different types of education so that people can actually do the things they are able to do. The effect would be to decouple the eligibility from a successful education, recognizing that there are different paths to success.

This objectification of the framework of educational policy suggests a return to the concept of education in its original form. At first sight, the separation of any particular purpose creates the appearance of an odd detachment from the world, but this truth was due to the well-intentioned view of first letting individuals find themselves before learning to serve other ends.

## THE SKEPTICS: ROLL BACKWARD INTO THE PAST

Some stand in opposition to the turn toward competence, most present arguments, and some revert to polemics like "the competence approach is a secret plan to produce illiterates" (Liessmann 2016, p. 131*ff*.). The flags of subjects and disciplines are waved, each featuring its own logic, which makes it necessary to differentiate the corresponding design of content mediation.

One of the spokespeople for this movement is Austrian philosopher and essayist Konrad Paul Liessmann, whose publications warn of the pending "illiteracy." He assigns responsibility for this state to the general education policy—especially, the current focus on competence. He condemns this approach by claiming a tie to the "disappearance of knowledge" (ibid., p. 45*ff*.), which is somehow now being withheld.

In its place, people are being fed "a diet of general abilities" (ibid., p. 45)—a trend in which Liessmann finds no pleasure. He is suspect of the competence approach—supposedly, a seamless takeover from economics—and conceals from his readers the discussions of competence theory by Chomsky, Habermas, and many other proponents of modern educationalists and rather foments a suspicion that subsequently takes on the context of a gloomy conspiracy "to control access to the inwardness and related forms of preparedness" (ibid., p. 47).

Competence is used as a diversion of purpose to gain intimate control over the learner according to Liessmann. No wonder he vehemently defends the learner from such an attack on self-development. But this superficial criticism misses the central point of the competence orientation: Liessmann criticizes Potemkin constructs he himself proposes, instead of adding substantial value. In his linkage to competence theories, he remains fixed on Heinrich Roth in the 1960s. His most recent reference to Franz E. Weinert is, after all, twenty years later, and we must wonder how such an obsolete view can claim to provide a current argument on the question of competence.

You can search in vain for some reference to current research on the EU competence concept (cf. Heyse et al. 2015; Stroh 2016; Wanken 2016) or the effort to make academic programs more transparent and self-directed through the use of competence profiles. If we follow Liessmann, things are rotten from the beginning. It is possible that Liessmann only upholds what he knows and appreciates and is also deaf to the growing skepticism about the "mediation" of content as increasingly determined by brain and cognitive research—on the basis of evidence, not personal opinion.

His is a belated position to propose in the competence discussions, and it offers little in the way of orientation. In particular, Liessmann celebrates a claim of completeness but nowhere really shows how learners can prepare for the exponential growth of knowledge. This question also arises because Liessmann assumes that insight is a prerequisite for knowledge. Liessmann is justified in recalling that it is the fascination with something that creates commitment and strengthens the learner's effort to master it (cf. Liessmann 2016, p. 53).

But what exactly is he describing that is so different from the competence approach? It remains puzzling why Liessmann makes the assessment that competencies are merely "formal skills" (ibid.). Is he not aware of the constant effort to specify technical competencies? Has he missed the fact that discussions over "vocational competence" already try—through proper and formal processing—to define technical problems more accurately? What other way out of the trap of obsolescence does he propose to show beyond the polemic that does not even address the core. He writes:

Competence runs into a void. Those who only learn how to deal with knowledge, paradoxically, do not know what to do with knowledge because that implies having knowledge. Therefore, the view that there is a fundamental difference between recalling and understanding something is also invalid. (ibid., p. 55)

Such argumentation is self-centered: it rests on an assumption that leads to absurdity. The assumption suggests there is some reasonable proposition that only tasks students to learn how to handle knowledge. In reality, just as before, all learning structures are based on their content domains. Anyone who studies philosophy in Vienna is immersed in a different domain than someone who studies electrical engineering in Zurich.

The competence approach does not question this focus on domains. The key is the fact that knowledge is not the only thing acquired, but in the domains themselves a reinforcement of abilities must also take place. Ultimately, in dealing with problems of content, acquired competence is what guides lifelong learning along the path of rapid change processes.

In the learning process, neither the rejection of all reference to knowledge nor its dominance can guarantee the essential goal: the sustainable development and internalization of the abilities for self-structured and appropriate solutions to new kinds of problems, which are naturally encountered in such domains. It is, ultimately, not an "either/or" issue, but a didactic question that sparks the competence debate (cf. Arnold/Erpenbeck 2014).

However, it is not the misinterpretations and horror scenarios alone that Liessmann uses to illustrate the world of competence, but rather the questions he leaves unasked. For example, he shows us no way out of the madness of completeness; on the contrary, he leaves the impression that it does not exist at all. Although he is not entirely silent on this point, he strongly rejects any notion of a future "that no one knows" (ibid., p. 56). At the same time, he never asks the question of how to effectively prepare for an uncertain future. "Not at all!" is what we get from his argumentation. According to his views, there is too much talk about the simple fact that

- Children and adolescents must naturally acquire certain abilities in order to participate in the society. We hear "this was always the case, and so it is OK as it was."
- Moreover, we should not try a competence-oriented approach because the future is unknown and you could become enthusiastic and immerse yourself in useless subjects.

Liessmann puts it this way: "We have become too cowardly to profess to intellectual content that is of value in and of itself and knowledge and understanding of which satisfies beyond the current needs" (ibid., p. 56*ff.*). Such liberalism would be surprised if the learners in our schools volunteered to study the given content in depth. This is not the case, which is why this plea for freedom in education is actually not one. It is a plea for things to remain as they are; not to be reviewed for their productivity for the learners.

Liessmann does not know how boring and unproductive the school year is for many people, especially, as they are forced to deal with extravagant content that has no connection to them, their abilities, and their questions. He ignores the secret curriculum at many educational institutions, where learners are taught not to follow their own impulses, but to submit to the given curriculum.

Finally, is Liessmann totally unaware of the scandalously low sustainability of such administered education? Can we really move on with the daily routine in the face of an increasingly uncertain future and merely continue with content and even press it into ridiculous lesson plans, curricula, and module handbooks that enable only execution, but no in-depth appropriation?

This criticism of the competence orientation confronts us with a concept that has forgotten the future. Furthermore, it applies distorted images of what competence orientation actually is in the context of European education policy, as well as the findings from brain and cognition research. We hear only polemics, not clarification when philosophers like Christoph Türcke awaken the impression that concepts like "competence" or "inclusion" are merely based on "articles of faith" (Türcke 2016, p. 17).

Those who are persuaded by such commentary will be complicit in the degeneration of learners into programmed "competence cripples" (ibid., p. 19) and are participants in the terrible consequences these ideas will have in our schools and universities. Liessmann and Türcke are prophets of doom. Both introduce the "twilight"—Türcke speaks of the "teacher twilight" and Liessmann of the "subject twilight" (Liessmann 2016, p. 45*ff.*) and leave no doubt that they are using the metaphor of the dusk of a beautiful day.

But was this day actually a good one? Are the issues and problems that educational institutions in modern societies have to manage arising because of the debate about changing and redirecting the concepts of teaching and learning? Are social selectivity and low sustainability for which public education bears responsibility really trivial concerns? These are the impressions gained by reading the "twilight books." Such books ignore the real issues and explain away in short order the efforts to optimize public education for the actual problems. They represent an ideological, if not to say, a cynical position.

*Chapter 9*

# Self-Learning Requires Appreciation, Guidance, Stimulating Arrangements, and Support

The departure from a content-, input-, and teacher-oriented world is no walk in the park. It can only succeed if the teachers perceive themselves increasingly as learners and set off on the path to seeing the familiar as something new. This requires courage and self-examination. And, the task itself is not a challenge to be taken personally.

Many teachers are aware of this because they have had to experience the limits of their own teaching action only too often; they did not want—and found it difficult—to accept the disappointing explanation that forgetting the knowledge and the fading away of competencies are an inevitable result of the teaching-learning process, just like the Amen follows the church sermon. The history of education is full of efforts to improve the sustainability of what learners experience at educational institutions.

However, some always vigorously oppose the attempts to rethink learning as competence development and to reconsider the roles in the teaching-learning process. A question often heard is, "Are you telling me that the things I have been trying to do for the past twenty years, in part, are no good?" Others note: "After all, the customers at our educational institutions expect us to present and explain things to them, even if they forget much of it afterward!"

Such questions can only be answered by referencing professionalism: if educators see themselves as professionals, they strive to redirect their actions over and over again to match the latest insights of teaching-learning research, cognition research, and competence development research. They do not seek to retain the habits and routines they themselves have experienced and developed. Pedagogy is aware of the imperfections in the art, but there is no instance where we find a checklist for a lack of success, as we know it from other professional areas of our society.

**TEXTBOX   9.1**

By focusing more on guidance and support to the learner, teachers can help to make learning what it truly should be at its core: *a self-directed activity*.

## LEARNING SUPPORT: THE PROFESSIONAL FUNCTION OF SCAFFOLDING

Teacher education also has to engage more and more with today's professional focus. Simultaneously, such learning support and/or learner guidance must take modern competence development approaches followed in the field of human resource development into account. In turn, it addresses the participants as competent learning systems, able to assess their own learning needs and able to assume responsibility for the pursuit of their own learning paths. More rejection of input-oriented concepts is necessary and, if you will, more acceptance of a principled confidence in learner potential.

Also, reflecting system research and practice, a resource orientation provides insights into how systems evolve largely on their own, by activating the patterns they already have to interpret and react to the present environment. In this sense, our thinking, feeling, and acting appear, systemically, as relatively "closed." This means that although we learn and try out new ways, these attempts are always based on our previous abilities, which we begin to expand and change only when they no longer lead us to the desired success.

This also applies to learning and competence development. Learning assistants "know" you can never really "teach" another person. You can only support them in shaping their own useful and effective learning movements, which requires a different attitude and approach than teachers have traditionally been trained for in the past. Of course, there have always been teachers who know how to "pick up their students when they fall." However, "learning support" takes this idea further: it is more radical.

**TEXTBOX   9.2**

Learning support rejects the notion of "picking up" the learner and assumes that you can only really accompany the learner to where he/she is able to go on his or her own. The focus is on the learner's own resources.

They become the fabric that learners use to construct their own success. The learning outcome does not result from a subtle addition of subject matter or the teaching effort, but unfolds in the approach to the learner and whether or not the teachers' activities express a behavior or attitude that resonates. In this sense, resource-oriented guidance is always resonance-oriented. Specifically, the wise teacher must always ask the underlying question: how do I manage to enter into a resonant relationship with the learner?

As the teachers get better at finding resonance with learners, the learners will increasingly have to practice reflective learning. "Reflective learning" not only relates to the content to be learned but at the same time keeps sight of the learning process. Reflection is reinforced and developed by means of the portfolio concept. The portfolio invites the learners to document for themselves

- Where are you in the learning process?
- How did you get there?
- Who or what helped or hindered you?
- What formal and informal learning venues have you passed through?
- What goals and steps have you planned along the path to reach the—usually predefined—overall goal?

It is this change of focus toward indirect action that characterizes the essence of learning assistance. In the implementation, the teacher does not fall into idleness, but changes the direction of actions and intents. It is no longer about the direct—mediated—impact on the learner, but on providing diverse opportunities and practicing indirect teaching.

The idea is to develop the ability "to scaffold" what is principally a self-directed learning movement by the learners: *scaffolding*—a word that clearly illustrates the role of the learning assistants; they are the scaffolders for the construction work of the learners.

## LEARNING FROM COMPLEX TASKS

"Learning from complex tasks" represents a totally different logic than the completeness concept. It deals with typology, not completeness. The following questions have to be considered in task-oriented skills development

1. How can I design the self-directed process for learning projects with the students?
2. How do I deal with the increasing heterogeneity and different levels?
3. How can I specifically target the weaker students?

"Learning from complex tasks" entails deriving learning requirements directly from the material, with the role of the teacher fading more and more into the background. In the ideal case, these are self-explanatory and need no introduction or commentary from the teacher. At the same time, "learning from complex tasks" requires opportune situations. The learner must have the maximum freedom to move about in the learning room and the learning period.

This idea not only disables the traditional curricular ideas, but it also has a fundamental impact on the question of architectural design of educational institutions and the possible arrangement of learning opportunities. Do they still present themselves according to the basic functions of training, instruction, and control, or do they transform into service and wellness areas to accompany the individual development process?

## OPPORTUNITIES AND LIMITATIONS OF GOOGLE KNOWLEDGE

What does it mean for a society when the tendency for change in the development of the educational system ultimately rests on the question: How do teaching and learning functions change if the learners can access more with one or two simple mouse clicks than from the well-educated teacher or even from partially obsolete textbooks? A meaningful interpretation of this question requires a further differentiation of the concept of knowledge, one that looks at knowledge both as a (necessary) element of competence and as a (teacher independent) form of specialization. The more knowledge, as in the ability to have a critical view, emerges from evidence, expertise, and creativity, the greater the supportive impact of explanations, interactions, and guidance in an attendance setting.

In brief, the appropriation of evidence does not need encounters, but rather creative usage, further development, and critique! This renewed quest for a contemporary concept of knowledge is illustrated in table 9.1. It differentiates the various forms of knowledge with different criteria of observation being used as the starting point

- The increasingly common use of *Google knowledge* for self-study is largely because it is accessible knowledge. It enables an unprecedented level of current detail (keyword "evidence"), but without resulting in any automatic expertise: many details do not automatically result in coherent knowledge, especially if it is a product of mere surfing. Although the Internet increasingly offers access to learning platforms and other self-learning opportunities, which no doubt can initiate, stimulate, and shape a more in-depth

**Table 9.1. From Google knowledge to coherent knowledge**

| | *Observation criteria* | | | |
|---|---|---|---|---|
| *Evidence* | *Expertise* | *Creativity* | *Critical* | *Forms of appropriation* |
| . . . viable is what functions (i.e., helps to solve the problem) | . . . viable is what the debate with experts withstands | . . . viable is how past thinking patterns are transformed | . . . . viable is the critique of existing and replacement with new | . . . through explanation, interplay, and accomp- animent (formal settings) |
| . . . viable is what the contrary withstands | . . . viable is the consideration of different perspectives | . . . viable is what in Socratic dialogue is checked | . . . viable is what superiority the solution can bring | |
| . . . viable is what I with others argue | . . . viable is a broad knowledge base | . . . viable is what with clear concept works | . . . viable is what prospects for action are given | |
| . . . viable is what is thoroughly researched | . . . viable is what to date explanations are known | . . . viable is on what knowl- edge and epistemology it is based | . . . viable is what examples (in the situ- ation) have been tested | . . . through independent learning (distance- setting) |
| | | **Knowledge form** | | |
| Google knowledge | Coherent knowledge | Reflective knowledge | Designing knowledge | Enabling didactics (mixing knowledge) |

expertise, it should not be overlooked that no broad professional acceptance of status can emerge from such insular absorption alone.

- This is in contrast to *coherentist knowledge*, which is established by means of anchoring in traditional forms of knowledge. Coherent knowledge is an associated knowledge. It relies on comparisons of manifold explanations, which it accepts or goes beyond. The foundation is the diversity of per- spectives that are integrated into this knowledge and contain irreconcilable contradictions with attempts at resolution not yet realized. Coherent knowl- edge is the treasure chest of expertise. It is found in textbooks, dictionaries, and training or study documents and is accessible for self-study. However, when learning to deal with the contradictions, uncertainties, or even errors, it is worthwhile to observe experts performing such activity and make contact with them. These encounters have little to do with instruction, but much with interaction, questioning, and accompaniment.

- We do not acquire *reflective knowledge* just for ourselves, although a lot has been written about this in perception and cognitive theory. However, it is helpful to first look for adequate forms in protected learning rooms to experience these new insights. How can we deal with reality if it only reveals itself to us in our own—preferred—possibilities? One can always remain "faithful," repeating the same theses throughout life, evaluating and excluding the assessments of others as "absurd, unnecessary, or uncritical" (Pongratz 2014). The reflective power of such repetitions, however, is limited, as it does not lead us to the transformation of our own patterns of thinking, but merely to affirmation of the past, without entering into a "Socratic dialog" whose purpose is always self-enlightenment, not self-righteousness.
- Ultimately, *designed knowledge* is active knowledge par excellence. This type of knowledge allows you to depart from your own routines to be able to bring about solutions. This knowledge, therefore, can only be effectively acquired in contexts that are not entirely like those for self-learning. The development, evaluation, and explanation of new perspectives require personal feedback as well as interrelated perspectives through interaction and self-efficacy in exemplary trials.

This commentary shows that distance and presence are two equally relevant dimensions in a self-transformation. All forms of knowledge are relevant, but meeting and sharing are not needed in equal measures in order to connect to them. These thoughts imply that classroom teaching is indeed a common didactic setting, but by no means necessarily indicated for all appropriation steps in competence development. Much can be said for the use of a mixed degree of enabling didactic, as explained later in more detail with reference to the different forms of knowledge.

Appropriate or *viable* behavior in life and work situations requires very different knowledge. In some cases, there is a need for accurate information in order to assess facts and to know the surrounding circumstances. For this case, the factual knowledge that is required is increasingly easy to find in lexical and documentary knowledge bases as a result of developments in information technology. Wikipedia and the entire online world exist because the retrievability of information has become increasingly simple.

It has long been not merely about reference questions, which can be answered more or less authoritatively by a few mouse clicks. This reduces disputes over realities (example: "How is that the same as what Pythagoras said?"), and you can easily get more comprehensive information (examples: "Tell me, when did he live again" or "What do we actually need this for nowadays?").

The Internet facilitates access to research reports or texts that would otherwise not be available (e.g., classroom materials on Euclidian geometry). You can surf through the hits for your initial query and before you know it, you have learned more than you initially wanted to know. In terms of accessibility, timeliness, and correctness, this Google knowledge cannot be beat as was noted in a study commissioned by the magazine *Stern* to compare Wikipedia and Brockhaus back in the year 2007.[1]

Google knowledge should not be underestimated. The free access to knowledge fulfills an ancient dream "to teach all men everything," to quote the philosopher, theologian, and first didactic Johann Amos Comenius in the year 1657 (Comenius 2008). This overcomes the boundaries of knowledge that have shaped the differences in competences between man and nations for centuries, and it is no longer unusual for teachers in Asia to prepare with MIT documents from Boston or for African universities to more easily overcome the competence deficit by prioritizing their access to global knowledge.

The global democratization of access to information and knowledge is also changing the eligibility to higher educational degrees and what was historically a function of education. These changes highlight a relationship that has legitimized social inequalities in the past through exclusion and selective assignment of life chances. Manuel Castells outlines an alternative in his three-volume analysis of the information age with the following words:

> The dream of the enlightenment, that reason and science would solve humanity's problems, is tangibly close. . . . There is nothing that could not be changed through intentional and purposeful actions, since information is available and can rely on a basis of legitimacy. (Castells 2003, p. 411)

Besides timeliness, information also has a context and a relationship to other—contrary or supportive—information. Consequently, Google knowledge only becomes knowledge in the true sense if it is given a knowledge context in terms of coherence and can be examined and classified. If you already have a coherent knowledge base, googling can be substantially of more use than for someone who selectively uses Google and rarely gets beyond patchwork knowledge.

Expertise requires coherent knowledge, that is, clarification of terms, structural knowledge, an overview of agreed clarification levels over a century of discourse as well as relevance criteria with which information can be assessed and evaluated. The evidence is quite strong that these meta-forms of knowledge (= knowledge, how to know or how to get to know and that while there is no certain, there are well-secured forms of knowledge) will hardly result from surfing Wikipedia, although you can also find convincing articles criticizing the observation, knowledge, and epistemology.

But who uses the search engines to come to grips with themselves and the destructive side effects of their own belief structure? Surfing seems to be a gesture that accesses and deals with knowledge more to affirm than to question. It promotes the "know it all" over the systematic "refutation attempts" that stem from coherent knowledge (Popper 1974, p. 106).

## REJECTING COMPLETENESS COMPLETELY

The crucial issue in an open-content world—in light of the different forms of knowledge, each with its own particular characteristics for the appropriation and development of competence—is not completeness, but competence. This is not achieved simply by the appropriation of knowledge; reflection and shaping skills are also necessary. In this sense, someone who has knowledge competence is said to have the knowledge and abilities to enable them to critically, in an open-minded way, deal with the levels of social progress regarding knowledge.

Such knowledge competence enables a person to perform "the research, appropriation, and evaluation as well as the management and sharing of information" (Arnold 2010, p. 36). This requires a special wisdom. Martin Lehner recalls William James's formula "wisdom is the art of recognizing what to overlook" and proposes:

> The following applies to every subject: Content can be provided in various dose concentrations. If the learning objectives, schedules, and target groups are defined, the correct content dosage can be found. As the framework conditions change, the dosage also changes. Basically, this is all about adjusting the concentration of the content and giving preference to a selection of essential content and statements. . . .
>
> If you follow the theory that "less is more," you are not merely bundling content, but also reflecting on it. Selecting content is a demanding activity that requires professional expertise while at the same time advancing it. (Lehner 2013, p. 39*ff.*)

To a certain extent, knowledge competence presupposes what it aspires to, that is, a reciprocal structure of expectations that initially overwhelms linear thinking. The different forms of knowledge have very different roles in the development of this competence. While coherent knowledge gradually evolves from examining, weighting, and categorizing information as well as critical discourse, Google knowledge is limited by a more rapid access and compression of information.

Coherent knowledge presupposes an internal regulatory framework that is not the result of broad-based use of information, but only from the development of subject matter competence. This form of knowledge must be initiated, accompanied, and supported. It requires the critical inquiry, interjection, and a refusal gesture that eludes the additive search mode of googling and looking up meanings.

Those who look things up usually have an idea they are trying to prove and illustrate: unlike a reflective search that looks in depth at ambiguities to wrestle with meanings and concepts, all for the purpose of leaving the expected understanding behind and perfecting the habit of acknowledging your own lack of understanding—just as the famous Socrates quote "*oika ouk eidos*" says: "I know that I do not know" (cf. Böhme 1988). Coherent knowledge is about learning to understand more and more, how to orient yourself, to assert yourself, and gradually to discover viable forms of reality construction.

The development and advancement of coherent, reflective, and shaped forms of knowledge results in the necessity to arrange irritating doubts, to insist on conceptual clarity and coherent positioning as well as on dealing with questionable contexts—a didactic challenge that is hardly achieved by googling alone. Although an enabling didactic considers the "impossibility of goal-oriented intervention" (Mohle/Seidl 2008, p. 269) and, consequently, the impossibility of mediation, it still relies on the competence-building effect of critical questioning (cf. Roth/Lück 2010).

This "self-inclusive observation" (cf. Varela et al. 1992, p. 54) increasingly breaks down the theoretical truths of the materialists and realists of this world and "(changes) the self-understanding in the mind of the analytic learner as the tangle of representations involving the learner is slowly unraveled by analysis" (ibid.).

---

**TEXTBOX   9.3**

Contexts for a self-directed learning and a "self-inclusive reflection" can be initiated by the successful expansion of the teaching arrangement as a "heaven full of questions" (Beilfuß 2015).

---

Even if it is difficult to prioritize competence-oriented concerns about the actual outcome into our education policies, there is no way to get away from the container images in the medium and long term. Education is not a possession, but an individual asset. An educated person demonstrates to us the ability to strive for appropriate solutions for novel problem situations. Staying in schools, colleges, or adult education centers for years *can* be helpful if it encourages people to engage in self-initiated, clarifying search movements and more detailed reflection.

However, the mere completion of a ready-made curriculum does not guarantee such a period of education. Such curricula are committed to the image of completeness, which arises from different motives:

- First, there is the idea that what is regarded as "binding" knowledge and ability in a society or community can be canonized. The use of the term "binding" is always controversial: while on one hand, Erich Weniger spoke of the "struggle of mental powers," on the other hand, he classifies it as regulatory duty off the publicly responsible authorities. Completeness becomes a compromise.
- The experts in the respective subjects and disciplines have fairly precise ideas about what belongs to the indispensable pool of professional expertise and what does not. The efforts to define a technical foundation (as opposed to add-on interests) have remained stuck in programmatic detail in almost all disciplines—perhaps, because the experts involved in preparing lesson plans and curriculum commissions are usually a party to the add-on interests, rather than the foundation.

## NOTE

1. Cf.    www.computerwoche.de/Wikipedia-laesst_brockhau:s_als_aussehen, 1849919 (visited February 21, 2016).

*Chapter 10*

# Skills Development Requires a Guide for Educational Institutions

The greater pedagogic sensitivity to the growing role of informal learning in acquiring competencies is accompanied by a greater awareness of the framework of institutional education. We question whether these frameworks encourage, engage, and support the learner or do they confront them with limitations, impositions, and nontransparency? This is the de-masking of a hidden curriculum of institutionalized and administered education, which fulfills the important functions of selection, certification, and regulation of access in our eligibility society.

It also ensures public responsibility for educational opportunities in life, while it also confronts the learner with a context in which mechanisms other than self-organization are at work. "Why should I get better at self-direction and try to optimize my self-study and my personality if I am forced to meet the external demands of an examination board?"—a question that expresses concern and nurtures doubt about the viability of a new learning culture.

For sustainable change to succeed in the direction of self-organization and the sustainable learning, it is essential to design educational institutions according to the provisos of self-organization. In addition to the way it is managed and developed, the focus has to be on organizational learning. Learning organizations are clearly differentiated from institutions that are primarily defined by their hierarchies, their responsibilities, and regulations.

The learning organization focuses on its own strategic change by exploring and reinforcing concepts that embody the concept of self-structured learning and sustainable competence development. These concepts include

- reinforcement of decentralized responsibility (keyword: (semi)autonomous schools),

- proactive as well as inclusive forms of leadership,
- a caring atmosphere also open to feedback,
- team-building and a modern learning culture,
- continuous transformation, and
- rational observations, documentation, and analysis of outcomes (e.g., based on performance indicators).

At the same time, there has to be an expansion of the accountability profiles of educators. They are not responsible only for the success of the core processes of "education" and "instruction." The basic functions for which they share responsibility also include the design and further development of the organization and certain aspects of human resource development. Essentially, "If you want to improve the teaching, you must do more than improve the teaching!" (Rolff 2007, p. 15)

These additional responsibilities go well beyond the teaching focus. While it is still useful or perhaps essential for school executives to be individuals who have a wealth of experience in everyday teaching, we cannot automatically assume that such experience alone is enough to actually master the complex requirements of strategic school development.

Executives in educational institutions today must be able to demonstrate more than just success as a teacher. Professional competence in the areas of human resource and organizational development is needed and you must also be able to justify and design a pedagogic profile for your school (refer to figure 10.1).

Let us turn now to the core processes of teaching and educational development. Basically, although the term "lesson development" indicates more than

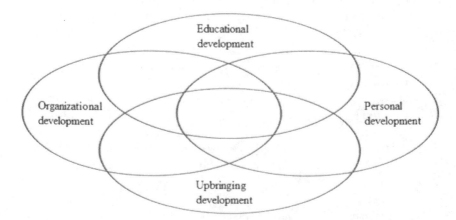

**Figure 10.1.   Aspects of school development**

just a guarantee to provide instruction and a desire to make the lesson itself more effective, the real education issues are all too often passed off as being a topic for the mothers and fathers with reference to the home. Such restraint fails to recognize that in terms of their individual identity development, newcomers are by no means "ready" when they reach the age to enter school.

Schools are the place where psychosocial disadvantages can be recognized and compensated. For some, school is also the first social environment where they receive real attention, reinforcement, and recognition. Lesson development is therefore based on professional concepts of personality development—in essence, the very core of successful education. School administrators have the task of profiling the program of their school as an educational program and linking it to the professional consciousness of the actors with respect to the criteria of sustainable competence development.

To develop schools as learning organizations, it is also important to target the strategic possibilities of human resource and organizational development. Schools are increasingly becoming a social organization in which professionals work together to perform their duties—continuously improving and looking for the most effective ways. They use team-building methods and continuously challenge their staff as they review the impact of their activities.

Learning organizations do not limit themselves to the administration of provisions, but rather are guided by vision, strategic options, and valid performance indicators. They ensure the quality of their programs as well as the quality of their cooperation and outcomes. In addition to continuous evaluation, the use of counseling and supervision are self-evident dimensions in the development of a learning organization.

Sustainable school development requires school directors to pursue continuing education to become better leaders. School directors today need professional as well as individual skills to enable them to have a deep understanding of the social logic. Certainly, leaders who strive for proper and sustainable evolution in their organization must learn how organizational power generates its own momentum, which has little in common with the "face-to-face interactions based on communication among those present" (Kühl 2016, p. 26).

Pedagogic leadership skills have a basis in self-reflection. The actors need more than a mere understanding of how the cognitive and emotional mechanisms of their own perception tend to express—transparently—the principle of preservation ("I want to stay as I am!"). They must also be practiced in leaving their obvious response behind; in particular, this refers to the following false self-assurances

- spontaneous assessments of the other person without always being aware of the effects of a self-fulfilling prophecy,

- overlooking the effect that we can only see the world and others as we are, that is, as suggested to us by our very own experiences,
- settled judgments that determine our attitude toward life that usually spring from an emotional construction of reality,
- skipping the self-reflection loop, which leads us to question immediate impressions and evaluations in terms of what they may be causing us to remember about ourselves, and
- missing the fact that it is precisely the situations that make it difficult for us and push us to the limit of our patterns that can challenge us to develop and make the difference become our friend (Arnold 2016, p. 122).

The further education of school executives enables them to become the shakers and movers of school development and inherently refers to a complex personal transformation for those in positions of responsibility. No one is a born leader, but you can become one. As this task shows, it requires a willingness to reflect on your own ideas about school, instruction, learning, change, and so on.

This willingness is what enables leaders to see and shape new opportunities for change—not just those that fit their own beliefs (held because they have them, not because they have proven "correct" after a thorough examination). Simply training pedagogic leaders in new management or leadership methods will always remain superficial, unless an effective way of influencing their attitudes is found.

## A QUESTION OF ATTITUDE

Systemic thinking, feeling, and acting represent a special attitude toward a world that seems to slip away the more resolutely a person "does something" based on his or her own explanations, descriptions, and assessments of the situation. The practitioner of systemics is aware of the complexity of the world and is a decided opponent of the simple if-then models. Such mechanistic models that view the world like a machine present an image of the world as an interaction of several systems.

Our inner images (cf. Hüther 2006) also tend to tell the story of our own experiences, fears, and suspicions—a statement expressed long ago in the Talmud: "We do not see the world as it is, but as we are!". We cannot completely suppress our inner images because they speak out on their own, and they often stand in the way, defining our inner monologues, and hinder our ability to enter a relationship: we are then in contact with our own assumptions and cares, but not with the other party, as he or she really is or could be.

Self-reflection in your thinking and acting will make you less inclined to base your actions on your own impression to the exclusion of all others. Rather, you will consider alternatives and deliberately try to find other interpretations of the events (e.g., among your employees). Overall, your attitude will be less "unilateral" (motto: "I am the observer who evaluates and shapes!") and more "flexible" (motto: "I observe the effects of my actions and then act accordingly!").

Systemic as used in this discussion means oriented toward the effects on the other party: leaders with this attitude, in principle, are actually closer to what moves the other party (whose development is of the leader's concern). Fundamental to such systemic thinking, feeling, and acting is open-mindedness toward what the other person either accepts or rejects. Systemic leaders know that good intentions alone are no guarantee for success. The same applies to the optimal—or even professional—design of your own interventions. Quality alone does not determine whether the other party will act on the proposition or not.

Systems professionals seek the most varied and stimulating designs for propositions; they do not believe in a mechanistic logic to determine what is actually achievable or even enforceable (impacts and outcomes). Increased effort may often lead to the opposite effect. Systems professionals know about these tendencies and the "blurring" that occur in complex and dynamic contexts. Such interrelated structures are characterized by circular causalities or even paradoxical situations that cannot be reliably controlled or even shaped.

Teachers and managers are well-advised to step back some distance from their own actions to observe the pattern in their actions. Self-distancing is not necessary so you can give up on the past—which is seldom successful—but so that you can expand and vary your own teaching and leadership style. No single leadership style is "right" or "wrong"; they are just extreme types with thinking, feeling, and action on the part of managers condensed to the extreme.

Emotions guide our beliefs: we "feel" when our explanations, interpretations, or reactions are justified and appropriate. An inner emotional balance signals "coherence," and then we cannot do otherwise but think, feel, and act the way we do. Although we experience an inner balance in such moments, this balance is our own internal event—usually with little reference to what the other person really meant or intended. We willingly "assume" the other person's intentions, as expressed through his or her behavior, to be exactly what we have imagined in our inner drama of such cases.

Emotional self-reflection is fundamental to cognitive guidance. Leaders need to know that their own minds are ready to take control of their interpretations and behavior in certain situations, and they must gradually be "allowed" to experience how it feels to *not* indulge this inner readiness, but to choose another way.

## LEARNING ORGANIZATIONS

The idea of organizational learning includes a new, constructivist dimension, that is, the extracurricular or interdisciplinary learning of the employees, the colleagues, or the teams. The issue is not about technical issues in the learning process, but rather initiating an ability to "rethink." Peter Senge describes this ability as "metanoia" (= rethink): "The learning organization is a place where people continuously discover that they create their own reality" (Senge 1996, p. 22).

Peter Senge develops the idea of "mental models," which every member of an organization has. These models determine perceptions, guide behaviors, and to a large extent whether and to what degree change and innovation will be supported or blocked:

> Specifically, new insights are generally not implemented because they contradict deep-rooted inner notions about the nature of things—ideas that tie us to familiar ways of thinking and acting. We must learn the discipline of managing mental models to bring to the surface our inner notions about the essence of things in order to review and improve them—a management discipline and a major step along the way to becoming a learning organization. (ibid., p. 213)

However, this perspective on mental models or the inner images that guide our thinking, feeling, and acting ahead of any reflection has its problems. What many now see as the possibility to have "everything on the table" also raises the risk of an overly meshed surveillance of the details.

Are we suddenly to make our most personal corners of thinking and our prejudices and experiences part of the operational interests? Is the learning organization the ultimate transparent organization? Is this transparency on track to creating the total organization in which everything becomes transparent, visible, and controllable? Would this not be an organization of completely transparent and visible employees? How is this totalitarianism compatible with an employee focus and the company's requirement to develop self-confident employees capable of independent actions? These risks cannot be completely eliminated, but they only occur when the "management of mental models" or the "transformation of interpretations" is introduced as a compulsory program in the old manner, perhaps even with the old technocratic dogma that mental models are "modifiable" (perhaps, like the term "management" as suggested by Peter Senge).

Ultimately, it is up to management to set the criteria for whether this modification was successful. Before this sensitive level in the transformation of interpretation patterns can be achieved by the company leadership and in human resource development, it is absolutely necessary to leave the transformation itself in the realm of voluntary self-action. The necessary strategies seem paradoxical.

---

### TEXTBOX   10.1

To achieve what is necessary (the "transformation of interpretation patterns") today, educational institutions and societies must enable (i.e., provide, finance, and professionalize) voluntary and open processes for self-reflection while not knowing for certain what the "outcome" will be.

---

You must pay particular attention to your basic patterns of interaction and those of others. You must free yourself from the myth of objectivity ("stay objective!") and give credence to the general fact that all interaction and cooperation have the dimensions of content as well as individual or personal relationship components. Often, working groups will argue fiercely about "the matter" because the members no longer "get along" personally with each other. How many good proposals were "cut down" with factual arguments because they were offered by an unpopular colleague or an unpopular executive?

It appears that we are unable to examine the facts with "impartiality" because as thinking, feeling, and acting individuals, we are fundamentally "biased." Aware of such a two-faced nature of our interactions (simultaneity of content and relationship aspects), we are basically required to de-escalate conflicts and discussions. This is best achieved by not immediately taking sides, rather by first analyzing the individual suggestions based on data and verifiable facts. In this way, leadership also contributes to a climate in which, in principle, every proposal is thought to be worthy of examination.

Over the years, the company "learns" that it does not depend on the social support that can be mobilized, but on the substantive quality of the arguments. This "objective orientation" form of leadership is difficult to "master," and it should not be realized in a way that the leader comes across as being a cold and rational actor of last resort for business decisions at the expense of remaining unloved and socially isolated.

On the contrary, for all outward appearances, the tendency must be to manage the somewhat annoying but "normal" fact that people just cannot help but see factual issues "passionately" and "emotionally." It is also important not to be deceived and affected by emotions. Leaders should not see themselves as the last instance for objectivity, but as a process-responsible actor, in the sense of de-escalation and argumentation.

## BEYOND THE CHALLENGE OF PREPARATION

It is no longer just idle talk to point out the escalating obsolescence of knowledge; rather it is based on multiple proofs of an unsettling view of the future. Whether this is taken up in many dramatic descriptions is open for discussion, but such assessments should not be overlooked.

Paradoxically, the path to the knowledge society seems to be linked to a change of attitude and a relativization of knowledge itself, a trend that also fundamentally effects school curricula.

What has historically been a codified supply of content or educational material that had to be prepared as a didactic curriculum and appropriated and "stored" by the learners can, in almost every subject area, hardly be defined today as a "binding" stock of material knowledge for the medium and long terms. Although secondary education and continuing education institutions are certainly more affected by this erosion of knowledge than primary schools, the scientific training institutions must also ask the question whether "retention training" can really remain the leitmotif of our educational system in the future, especially as knowledge is becoming obsolete more rapidly and can also be stored and retrieved more easily external to the learner.

The answer is clearly, "No, it cannot." The concept of retention training must be replaced by one of strength training or with the advancement of methods and social skills development. In place of short-term retention (and forgetting in the medium and long terms), the goal is the sustainable development of competence. Andreas Müller, a Swiss educator proposes:

> Knowledge demands operating instructions: Work methods, teaching-learning, strategies for creative problem solving, thinking and acting in terms of goals and options, sensitizing for networking and interactions, self-discipline, team and consensus building, helpful assistance, self-responsibility, self-initiative, self-activity replace being instructed. . . .
>
> Sustainable learning opens paths to the future. The principle of sustainability takes aim in two different directions. One of these concerns the sustainability of the learning patterns. This refers to lifelong learning as a basic concept of modern living. The other involves the sustainability of the learning outcomes. What this means is a permanent expansion of competence with regard to individual success in life. (Müller 1999, p. 11)

A classic pedagogic thought, which also determined the discourse on vocational training for a long time, is that schools and training organizations have to "pass on" the knowledge, skills, and abilities developed by past generations to the next generation to ensure further development of society. In effect, education and training provide for the "accelerated" development of the individual and guarantee that personal and social development advances from generation to generation.

Such intellectual thought remains valid for as long as the "supply" of knowledge, skills, and abilities to be passed on is more or less stable. In light of the continuing accumulation of knowledge, however, it becomes more relevant to ask what skills will still be relevant five, ten, or fifteen years from now. In addition, the ability to communicate and to solve immediate problems is at least as crucial today as the availability of the technical expertise. In the new world of work relationships, expertise and know-how can usually lead to productivity only through cooperation as well as self-directed and networked activity.

This continues a trend that has been observed in modern labor markets for over forty years. The pattern marks a significant extension of qualification requirements to extra-functional or extracurricular skills and knowledge. The relationship between general education and vocational training will be redefined as many of these qualifications are more general, that is, not job-specific, even though they are acquired most sustainably in the occupational activities.

Leadership and cooperation will also have to change. There is a growing insight by the operational management in many companies that authoritarian and hierarchical corporate structures and patterns are no longer adequate to achieve sufficient cooperation and the quality necessary for survival in dynamic and highly competitive markets. These developments indicate that companies with operational qualifications expanding in the direction of "original" training goals, for example, self-empowerment, independence, and critical abilities—assuming these are really seen as a necessity and are genuinely aspired to—will (have to) engage in a new dimension of human resource development.

They will prepare for just the opposite of the classic view of general and vocational education. Human resource development (i.e., training and advanced education) takes on features of personality development whose expression was normally not allowed by operational controls. The expression that there is no such thing as "a little bit" of self-empowerment—similar to "you cannot be a little bit pregnant"—illustrates the inseparable nature of education.

Companies that embark on the path of advanced qualification—if they wish to use the functional aspects of such a qualification—must also promote and develop the aspects of self-empowerment that benefit the learner and that learners can use to oppose operational objectives and improve their position within the company—an extremely important sociopolitical dimension in the transformation of vocational learning cultures.

By no means do all companies fully commit to such expanded qualification and the development of their cooperative structures, so it is also of little further use to speculate on the percentage of change to organizational learning. However, the potential for change is revealed and triggered at the margins of the empirically provable. In particular, it is the ever-closer cycles of change in the average aging of technical knowledge that are fundamentally calling into question the *preparation and retention* characteristics of the traditional learning cultures.

Particularly affected are those of prevocational training (vocational schools, universities, in-company training, etc.) where the guiding concept of "mediated on-hand knowledge" is turned on its head! The same applies to the traditional demarcation of general education and vocational training. The substance of the abilities that make up the more advanced, increasingly involved competencies (problem-solving, self-directed, etc.) is clearly a general or personality-forming substance.

The erosion of the stock of specialized know-how and the emergence of more open forms of cooperative problem solving in the work processes replace the security—assumed or actual (motto: "We already know what is important")—with a new *insecurity* or *uncertainty*. The labor market and occupational research predictions are of a general nature and not very specific with regard to medium- and long-term development trends. We read that the trend curve in the service occupations is rising as the number of jobs for unskilled workers is declining.

Yet we are not informed—or are suspicious of the information we do get—about what kind of job activities are to be expected in a medium-term framework and to what extent. Even less information is provided on the technologies to be developed in these workplaces so that we cannot clearly determine what expertise we need to convey to students, apprentices, and employees today in order to prepare them as specifically as possible for their professional future.

The sound of the cracking illusion of being able to curricularize content completely goes largely unheard. Yet expertise can be curricularized only to a very limited degree, that is, identified and bundled under well-founded anticipation of the expected "later use situations" (Robinsohn) for today's teaching-learning processes. Similarly, we see the failure of our traditional "more-of-the-same concept" of educational policy in terms of sustainability.

The question to be asked now is whether we should not look for solutions elsewhere to effect a reform and further develop our education systems—somewhere where there is light and not in the dusk where we think we lost our solution. In other words, perhaps the solution to the disillusionment in technical education caused by the obsolescence problem does not lie in technical education itself, but rather outside the technical education.

Possibly, given the rates of obsolescence in knowledge, we may not need "extra education" at all, but more "identity education," more serenity, more depth, more self-empowerment, more time for search movements and skills development. This is the direction of the current attempts to define key competencies as serious targets in vocational training and to initiate the corresponding action-oriented approaches. At the same time, greater distance from the completeness requirements of traditional curriculum concepts is achieved, and the focus is more on the idea of process-oriented education.

In summary, as a result of the increasing "openness" in the development of requirements, curricular illusions of a hasty training qualification must increasingly be abandoned. The same holds true for the illusion that what is taught is learned, and only learned if taught. A different learning culture is needed, one which is also accompanied by a change in the focus of human resource development. It can no longer be primarily about adapting individuals to the change, but rather about shaping the preconditions for teaching the learners to develop and support their own ability to change.

The learners must be able to express their own potential during the learning process. That is why the didactic methodology of the teaching process is gaining significance as a supplement to the long-standing view that placed content in the foreground: the journey is the goal. For this reason, the learning cultures of companies and schools in our society must become more methodical and more characteristic of teaching.

In the context of corporate socialization, in place of a top-down structuring, employees have to be systematically empowered to build their own experience forming realities before any training that will eventually equip them to respond appropriately in serious situations in the workplace can occur. This means not waiting for solutions to problems to come "from above," but acting—from below—by proposing solution models and trying your own solutions.


## DO NOT LEAVE OUT THE FACTS, EXPAND ON THEM!
## FIGHT THE DEMONS OF POPULISM

The contemporary talk of a post-factual age trivializes what is in truth a regression in the enlightened use of reason. This section presents a relatively detailed look at the "world view of the function of scientific knowledge" (Vollmer 1991) and examines the question if and to what extent behavioral

sciences like pedagogy are demanded to revive the old—humanistic—
thought, according to which the truth viably shows itself only through science.

In our attempt to develop a contemporary understanding of science, we
must not stop with facts, but try to look beyond the evidence and familiarize
ourselves with our own mechanisms of constructing reality. This is the core
of self-reflection in learning, and this has a factual and meta-factual orientation. It is immune to post-factual regression, which is actually a reversion
into pre-factual worldviews. But be cautious with all legitimate degradation
of pre-factual constructions. We will find that we also have to admit that we
are more pre-factual than we would sometimes like to think.

## How factual is reality?

According to the evolutionary cognitive theory of the German physicist
and philosopher Gerhard Vollmer (born 1943), the forms of description and
explanation of the worldview throughout human civilization have gradually
evolved—from a preponderance of magical explanations to the theologic-
mystic and philosophical to the scientific—each step an improvement in
terms of the consistency, collective understanding, and verifiability of its
findings. As an evolutionary epistemologist, Vollmer assumes a correspon-
dence between environmental conditions and cognitive faculties when he
states:

> Our cognitive ability is a product of evolution. The subjective cognitive struc-
> tures fit the world because they have evolved in the course of evolution in
> adaptation to this real world. They agree (partially) with the real structures
> only because such a correspondence was necessary for survival. (Vollmer 1988,
> p. 102)

Vollmer's analysis sounds plausible (refer to figure 10.2), but it also exposes
Vollmer as a reflective thinker: he does not relativize the perception, and he
would never agree with Humberto Maturana, who never tires of pointing out
in his biologic cognitive theory that humans construct the world only according to their own terms and conditions and in agreement with the output from
their sensory organs (cf. Maturana/Varela 1987).

In a recent essay, Maturana and colleagues suggest that the millions of
different forms of "operational coherence" have not been developed and
preserved in the "evolutionary drift" (Maturana et al. 2017) because they
are "right" or were required to ensure survival—especially as it is not yet
clear whether we will count as a "compatible" or "incompatible civilization"
(ibid.). Rather, the individual person is merely an "observer and user" of his
or her environment as Wolfgang Neuser writes.

| Evidence base | Stages of professional world perspective | Example: personality development | Description | Explanation value | Inner consistency | Outer consistency | Testable | Predictable | Configurable |
|---|---|---|---|---|---|---|---|---|---|
| Perspective | Magical | Forces of nature or ancestors are expressed in the individual and determine their destiny. | X | ? | | | | | |
| | Theologically mythical | People "serve" in essence a higher purpose through expressing the divine meaning of life. | X | X | ? | | | | |
| | Philosophical | People are rational beings whose understanding of the world is rational and can be shaped. | X | X | X | ? | | | |
| | Scientific | The conditions and mechanisms of that shape identity and competence are identifiable, measurable, and publishable. | X | X | X | X | ? | | |
| Stance | Epistemology | People can not see the world as it is, but rather as we see it. | X | X | X | X | X | ? | |
| | Self-reflexive | People see themselves and the world through their biographically proven assumptions. | X | X | X | X | X | X | ? |
| | Operative | People change their world by changing themselves. | X | X | X | X | X | X | X |

Figure 10.2.   Development of world perspective based on pedagogic concepts (Vollmer 1991)

As such, we merely move on pre-poured foundations that accustom us to assume "a world around us based on causal relationships" (Neuser 2017), which is why we welcome a factual orientation without which nothing is possible, but also we are well-advised not to lose sight of the fact that these cannot be produced without cognitive opportunities and routines. An evidence orientation is an advanced cognitive habit—advanced, but a habit nevertheless. Consequently, its effectiveness must be questioned—according to the slogan of the American pragmatists: "Truth is what works."

What do these indications have to do with pedagogy and its scientific nature? The answer is easy and yet disillusioning

- It is easy because it illustrates that we have to overcome the magical, theologic-mystic, and philosophical interpretations in professional teaching in order to ensure that factual references, collective understanding, and examination replace mere opinion and prejudices. There is no alternative but to reference the evidence when we have the facts about something. The actions of teachers today are not entirely free from magical-mythical explanations, as shown by the success of teaching guidebooks that, without any reference to evidence, celebrate the positive effects of discipline in the classroom or call for more value orientation as if they already had a reliable clarification of the if-then relationships in the formation of values and attitudes in children and adolescents. If we inwardly give this the nod in the face of such calls, it only shows how strongly we are still caught up in magical-mythical delusion of omnipotence.

• Separating ourselves from mystic-theologic concepts is difficult because they have a continued effect to this day and have given us the ideas that we still use to designate what we otherwise would not be able to designate. For example, this applies to the concept of education, which has its roots in the mythical theology of the Middle Ages and still works today with image-of-God promises, without knowing "what manner of spirit he is" (Lucas 9:55). In searching for the anchor to our worldview in scientific pedagogy the question asked is: Does "education" exist today because we discovered it or is it independent of our discovery? Another good question is: What are we doing if we are using a traditional category for our empirical explanation of fact? We only find what we have a concept for already.

The focus on facts provides us with a red line for an enlightened interaction with the world, and if we do not want to sink into the swamp of opinions of bygone times, we must neither retreat in the areas of science or teacher training, but rather counter with the professional maxim: "Every person has a right to their opinions, but not to their own facts!" Evelyn Roll used this quote from the deceased sociologist, diplomat, and U.S. senator Daniel Patrick Moynihan (Roll 2016) in the newspaper *Süddeutschen Zeitung*.

In the same edition of that paper, Jadoga Marinić appealed to those who pretend that culture is collapsing: "Don't be blinded by the arrogance of success" (Marinić 2016). These are two important reminders to look to facts and evidence for our worldview and social interactions. In the context of teacher training through a uniform science, the training in fact-oriented thinking and argumentation will remain strangely hollow unless we succeed in getting the future teachers to look behind the facts.

In short, we have to make them seek a meta-factual dimension in the spirit of Ludwig Wittgenstein, who said: "Just because something appears so to me, doesn't make it so!" In the context of applied cognitive theory, the better question to ask is: "What does the situation I am experiencing currently remind me of?"

## How effective is science?

We certainly have the logic and the rationale to dispute the validity of findings, to examine arguments, to weigh the counterarguments, and to decide when we cannot test reliably! But are we sure that the better arguments come to us and automatically lead us to change worldviews that are strengthened by experience? Do we not hold on to our cherished habits and hypotheses—even if all the evidence seems to prove us wrong?

Of course this is true, especially, in the areas of life that do not confront us with rationally calculable objects (such as the asteroid belt) and tend rather to condense to certainty from self-experienced practice. "Humans are creatures of habit," wrote Foucault, explaining why our *experiences* with objects are indispensable in determining the facts—especially, as we carry these concepts within us.

Can university teachers really switch to another form of teaching when told the current consensus among learning and brain research is that content cannot be taught? Especially, if they have simultaneously completed—and not without some success—their own learning biographies in instructional contexts that provided them with emotional certainty (motto: "It cannot have been in vain!").

Based on experience, pointing out that our own path to success is not set because of, but rather in spite of, the instruction we receive—since our brain does what brains do, namely, it appropriates new things, tries them out, and condenses them to develop expertise—is not a suitable means for effecting change in our own worldview because we cannot endure it. To this point, irritating comments are made by cognitive researchers that concern dismissing our rigidity in thinking, feeling, and acting as an "illusion of false causal attribution," which also clearly marks the professional limits of "exclusively" regarding scientific explanations.

This has been known ever since Diethelm Wahl proposed the *Konstanzer Wanne* (The Lake Constance Dip), yet only a few conclusions have been drawn from these findings. My thesis is: *Science is the effort to focus on facts, but not on the facts of the immediate case, but only on those facts that I can endure as a discerning observer.*

It has long been known that the explanation of complex—social—causal relationships requires not just an explanatory theory, but also a comprehensive faculty of reason. Additional criteria, namely the senses of reason, apply in the behavioral sciences. Behavioral sciences are concerned almost exclusively with "objects" that not only confront us externally, but also with those things we carry as a dense network of experience within us—upbringing, education, teaching, learning, leading, being led, and so on.

Professionalism, in the sense of reasonable actions with relevance to the facts, must therefore be able to expand to a meta-factual dimension, so as not to drown in the Constance Dip during the transition from technology to professional practice. To avoid this dip in our experience patterns, we must have the ability to question the effectiveness of our educational and teaching activities by opening an inner dimension.

## What to do? Views on reflection in (teacher) training

Genuine self-reflection in teacher training must serve to clarify pre-factual perspectives and ideas, but it must also recognize the self-limiting nature of simple facts about upbringing, education, teaching, and learning while providing an immunization against facile—but ineffective—factual references. Rather, by expanding your view of the world with a meta-factual dimension that allows you to deal with the fact that we do not perceive the world, we admit it, to paraphrase Gunther Schmidt.

First, an understanding of this self-referentiality of all observations, reasoning, and conclusions is needed to open the discourse to other constructions of reality. Student teachers who learn to think meta-factually understand that

- They cannot see the world as it is, but only as they are (again borrowing a clever thought from the Talmud).

  *In a professional context, they should recall the fact just because a particular student seems to be "difficult" does not automatically mean that is really the case.*
- Professionals always tend to judge themselves and the world through their assumptions (patterns of interpretation and emotion), which explains why it is that they always recognize prior experience and interpretations; actually, the professional "is constantly dealing with himself," as Manfred Spitzer writes.

  *In a professional context, he/she can constantly ask: What does the situation I am experiencing remind me of so that I may subtract these particular certainties from the given situation and allow it to appear the way it, de facto, wants to appear? This is an exercise for which educational hermeneutics has already provided substantial preparatory work.*
- Change can only be effected in the professional (teachers and managers) if they change themselves, that is, learn to give up or enrich their preferred worldviews, to say goodbye to their obvious interpretations—whether sitting on the edge or already in the Constance dip—and to practice repeatedly letting a new reality shine in.

  *In a professional context, you cannot "effect" anything, but you can ensure that something new and different can appear and "act" on that—that is how reality is constituted (by the way, not just in the fields of social sciences and the humanities).*

Based on my experience, reflective practices in teacher training and the meta-factual handling of a situation can produce more effective results. Science is not just a qualifying phase along the way to becoming a teacher (without taking the Constance dip), but has the chance to become a grounding element, enabling professionals to "always act in a way that gives them an increasing number of options," as the constructivist Heinz von Förster wrote. The meta-factual orientation on science provides the tools, namely self-reflection tools, with which we can accept and test these multiple options.

A teacher from northern Germany wrote:

> Since I started teaching, I have had a funny feeling about the setting (being responsible for the development of a group of 25, all the same age, in 45 minutes; I "produced" learning). Now, in the enabling didactic, I have found myself again. I have read Spitzer, Juul, Hüther, Holzkamp and others. . . . They have given voice and offered direction to my doubts. They have inspired me. In my role as a teacher, I am quasi developing or redesigning myself all the time.

That is all there is to it, and it is effective! That is quite a lot!

# Conclusion: The Outlook—Journey to the Age of Self-Structured Learning

Humanity is well-advised to be suspicious of manifestos or dogma-like texts. No positive experience has ever been gained by following them as their assumptions tend to fade away. The particular danger is when attempts to explain/understand the world are confused with the actual situation. The things that affect us and our interactions with others can only be sensed through clear self-reflection and courageous thinking, and ultimately, we have no absolute certainties.

We are observers who base our perceptions not merely on a rational view, but also on the emotional and cognitive foundation that we have available. Our view traces an image of the world not as it really is, but as we have learned to live with it! Things are not "true" just because we want them to be! We often miss the idea that "it could be entirely different!"

This advice is not to open the door to arbitrary thinking, feeling, and acting, but rather to advocate a slowdown. If we realize that we are part of a developing situation that continues without asking for our permission, then we can change our patterns of observation: we no longer see ourselves as photographers of some reality, but instead as its builder. We increasingly come to understand that we are seeing the world "as we are." What appears real to us passes through the lens of our assumptions, the ones through that we have learned to focus.

What seems real to us is what comes into our view and gains our attention. Everything else escapes from our view or is categorized as unreal or, perhaps even as "nonsense." Our selective gaze even overlooks evidence, misses opportunities, and holds us prisoner to a position—not arrogance—but supported by the assumption that *we* are the ones with access to contextual knowledge that others do not have. Such resolute thinking operates with short circuits of a special kind. It arrives without "self-inclusive reflection" (Varela et al. 1992) and beams itself into a position that promises more than it can deliver.

Still, when people are able to see through and move beyond the mechanisms that always hold their thinking, feeling, and acting in the same patterns, they are released from the pull of repetition and are more and more able to form a reasonable impression—even if this seems to question what our experience is letting us process. This movement is essential for any change in the learning culture of our society.

Teachers, school directors, and educational policy makers are entrusted to also consider evidence that contradicts the thinking habits, attitudes, and prejudices of broad sections of the public. In particular, this applies to the stubborn idea that

- the mediation of knowledge is possible and necessary,
- knowledge allows competence to develop, and
- teachers can effectively intervene in the cognitive and emotional patterns of the learners.

In contrast, insights provided by efforts to search for rational causal relationships suggest a departure from such assumptions by showing us the following

- Knowledge must be appropriated and (re)constructed by the learners themselves—always on their own terms in the sense of linked learning.
- Although knowledge is a key dimension in the development of competence and expertise, it alone cannot create competence, since we know people can be very knowledgeable and yet are still unable to do anything (cf. Arnold/Erpenbeck 2014).
- Teachers have no possibility to input or intervene in the self-organization of the learner, which is why pedagogic professionalism has to be reconsidered and practiced in the sense of learning guidance.

The more we succeed in opening the learning cultures in our society to such evidence, the faster we can leave behind us those concepts of instruction and interventionist teaching that have dominated education and the education sciences since well before the 1970s. This would mark the advent of the age of self-structured learning.

# Bibliography

Abel, G. (1998): Nietzsche: Die Dynamik der Welt zur Macht und die ewige Wiederkehr. 2., um ein Vorwort erweiterte Auflage. Berlin u. a: Walter de Gruyter.

Anderson, J. R. (1976): Language, Memory and Thought. Hillsdale, NJ: Erlbaum.

Arbesman, S. (2012): The Half-Life of Facts. Why Everything We Know Has an Expiration Date. New York: Penguin.

Argyris, C. (1997): Wissen in Aktion. Eine Fallstudie zur lernenden Organisation. Stuttgart: Klett-Cotta.

Arnold, R. (1997): Die Emergenz der Kognition. Skizze über Desiderata der Erwachsenendidaktik. In: Derichs-Kunstmann, K./ Faulstich, P./ Tippelt, R. (Hrsg.): Enttraditionalisierung der Erwachsenenbildung. Dokumentation der Jahrestagung 1996. Beiheft zum Report. Frankfurt a. M., S: Dt. Inst. für Erwachsenenbildung (DIE). 130–146.

Arnold, R. (2005): Autonomie und Erwachsenenbildung. In: Hessische Blätter für Volksbildung, 55, 1, S. 37–46.

Arnold, R. (2007): Aberglaube Disziplin. Antworten der Pädagogik auf das »Lob der Disziplin«. Heidelberg: Carl-Auer.

Arnold, R. (2010): Systemische Berufsbildung. Kompetenzentwicklung neu denken—mit einem Methoden-ABC. Baltmannsweiler: Schneider.

Arnold, R. (2011): Veränderung durch angewandte Erkenntnistheorie. In: Ders. (Hrsg.): Veränderung durch Selbstveränderung. Impulse für das Changemanagement. Baltmannsweiler: Schneider, S. 1–8.

Arnold, R. (2013a): Von der Veränderung des Fachlichen in Prozessen der Kompetenzreifung. In: Ders./Gómez Tutor/Menzer, C. (Hrsg.): Didaktik im Fokus. Baltmannsweiler: Schneider, S. 219–227.

Arnold, R. (2013b): Selbstbildung. Oder: Wer kann ich werden und wenn ja wie? 2., korrigierte Auflage. Baltmannsweiler: Schneider.

Arnold, R. (2013c): Wie man lehrt, ohne zu belehren. 29 Regeln für eine kluge Lehre. Das Lena-Modell. 2., unveränderte Auflage. Heidelberg: Carl-Auer.

Arnold, R. (2015): Bildung nach Bologna. Die Anregungen der europäischen Hochschulreform. Wiesbaden: Springer.

Arnold, R. (2016): Wie man wird, wer man sein kann. 29 Regeln zur Persönlichkeitsbildung. Heidelberg: Carl-Auer.

Arnold, R./Erpenbeck, J. (2014): Wissen ist keine Kompetenz. Dialoge zur Kompetenzreifung. Baltmannsweiler: Schneider.

Arnold, R./Gómez Tutor, C. (2007): Grundlinien einer Ermöglichungsdidaktik. Bildung ermöglichen—Vielfalt gestalten. Augsburg: ZIEL.

Arnold, R./Gómez Tutor, C./Prescher, T./Schüßler, I. (Hrsg.) (2016): Ermöglichungsdidaktik: Offene Fragen und Potenziale. Baltmannsweiler: Schneider.

Arnold, R./Lermen, M. (Hrsg.) (2013): Independent Learning. Die Idee und ihre Umsetzung. Baltmannsweiler: Schneider.

Arnold, R./Lermen, M./Günther, D. (Hrsg.) (2016): Lernarchitekturen und (Online) Lernräume. Bd. 2 zur Fachtagung »Selbstgesteuert, kompetenzorientiert und offen?!« Baltmannsweiler: Schneider.

Arnold, R./Neuser, W. (Hrsg.) (2017): Die Beobachtung des Wissens—Das Wissen des Beobachters. Annäherung an eine systemische Hermeneutik. Baltmannsweiler: Schneider.

Arnold, R./Nittel, D. (2015): Del déficit tecnológico a la autotecnología. In: Hernandez, F. J./Villar, A. (Hrsg.): Educación y biografías. Perspectivas pedagógicas y sociológicas actuales. Barcelona: Editorial UOC, S. 211–238.

Arnold, R./Siebert, H. (2006): Die Verschränkung der Blicke. Konstruktivistische Erwachsenenbildung im Dialog. Baltmannsweiler: Schneider.

Astin, A. W./Astin, H. S./Lindholm, J. A. (2011): Cultivating the Spirit. How College Can Enhance Students' Inner Lives. San Francisco: John Wiley & Sons.

Baethge, M./Baethge-Kinsky, V. (2004): Der ungleiche Kampf um das lebenslange Lernen. Münster u. a: Waxmann.

Beck, S. (2010): Vertrauen geschmolzen? Zur Glaubwürdigkeit der Klimaforschung. In: Aus Politik und Zeigeschichte, 32–33, S. 15–21.

Beilfuß, C. (2015): Ein Himmel voller Fragen. Systemische Interviews, die glücklich machen. Heidelberg: Carl-Auer.

Beise, M./Schäfer, U. (2016): Deutschland digital. Unsere Antwort auf das Silicon Valley. Frankfurt a. M: Campus.

Bell, D. (1975): Die nachindustrielle Gesellschaft. Frankfurt a. M: Campus.

Bittner, G. (2011): Das Leben bildet. Biographie, Individualität und die Bildung des Proto-Subjekts. Göttingen: Vandenhoeck & Ruprecht.

Bohm, D. (2011): Der Dialog. Das offene Gespräch am Ende der Diskussionen. 6. Auflage. Stuttgart: Klett-Cotta.

Böhme, G. (1988): Der Typ Sokrates. Frankfurt a. M: Suhrkamp.

Bolder, A./Epping, R./Klein, R./Reitter, G./Seiverth, A. (Hrsg.) (2010): Neue Lebenslaufregimes—neue Konzepte der Bildung Erwachsener? Wiesbaden: Springer.

Brater, M. (1988): Berufsbildung und Persönlichkeitsentwicklung. München: Verlag Freies Geistesleben.

Castells, M. (2003): Jahrtausendwende. Das Informationszeitalter. Opladen: Springer.

CEDEFOP (2012): Veraltete Qualifikationen—was tun? Der rasche Wandel des Arbeitsmarktes führt dazu, dass viele Arbeitnehmer von Qualifikationsverlust bedroht sind. Kurzbericht. Online verfügbar unter: www.cedefop.europa.eu/files/9070_de.pdf (Aufruf am 28.2.2017).

Comenius, J. A. (2008): Große Didaktik: Die vollständige Kunst, alle Menschen alles zu lehren. 10. Auflage. Hrsg. von A, Flitner. Stuttgart: Klett-Cotta.

Damasio, A. (2011): Selbst ist der Mensch. Körper, Geist und die Entstehung des menschlichen Bewusstseins. München: Siedler.

de Shazer, S. (2006): Das Spiel mit Unterschieden. Wie therapeutische Lösungen lösen. 5. Auflage. Heidelberg: Carl-Auer.

de Solla Price, D. J. (1974): Little Science, Big Science. Von der Studierstube zur Großforschung. Frankfurt a. M: Suhrkamp.

Dräger, J./Müller-Eiselt, R. (2015): Die Digitale Bildungsrevolution. Der radikale Wandel des Lernens und wie wir ihn gestalten können. München: DVA.

Ehmer, S./Regele, W./Regele, D./Schober-Ehmer, H. (2016): ÜberLeben in der Gleichzeitigkeit. Leadership in der »Organisation N. N.«. Heidelberg: Carl-Auer.

Ehrenberg, A. (2008): Das erschöpfte Selbst. Depression und Gesellschaft in der Gegenwart. Frankfurt a. M: Campus.

Emcke, C. (2016): Reden anlässlich der Verleihung des Friedenspreises des Deutschen Buchhandels, 23. Oktober 2016. Available at: https://www.friedenspreis-des-deutschen-buchhandels.de/sixcms/media.php/1290/Friedenspreis%202016%20Reden.pdf

Erpenbeck, J./Sauter, W. (2016): Stoppt die Kompetenzkatastrophe! Wege in eine neue Arbeitswelt. Wiesbaden: Springer.

Erpenbeck, J./von Rosenstiel, L. (2007): Vorbemerkung. In: Dies. (Hrsg.): Handbuch Kompetenzmessung. 2. Auflage. Stuttgart: Schäffer-Poeschel, S. XI–XIV.

Foucault, M. (2009): Die Regierung des Selbst und der andere. Frankfurt a. M: Suhrkamp.

Freire, P. (1985): Pädagogik der Unterdrückten. Bildung als Praxis der Freiheit. Stuttgart: Rowohlt.

Gabriel, M. (2013): Warum es die Welt nicht gibt. Berlin: Ullstein eBooks.

Gamm, H.-J. (1983): Materialistisches Denken und pädagogisches Handeln. Frankfurt a. M: Campus.

Göhlich, M./Wulf, C./Zirfas, J. (2014): Pädagogische Theorien des Lernens. Weinheim: Beltz.

Gomez, P./Probst, G. (1995): Die Praxis des ganzheitlichen Problemlösens. Vernetzt denken—Unternehmerisch handeln—Persönlich überzeugen. Bern u. a: Haupt.

Gunnlaugson, O./Sarath, E.W./Scott, C./Heeson, B. (2014): An Introduction to Contemplative Learning and Inquiry. In: Gunnlaugson, O./Sarath, E. W./Scott, C./ Heeson, B. (Hrsg.): Contemplative Learning and Inquiry across Disciplines. New York: SUNY Press.

Heintl, P./Krainz, E. E: (1994): Was bedeutet »Systemabwehr«? In: Götz, K. (Hrsg.): Theoretische Zumutungen. Vom Nutzen der systemischen Theorie für die Managementpraxis. Heidelberg: Carl-Auer-Systeme, S. 160–193.

Herwig M./Völpel, A./Zwecker, C. (2014): Nachhaltige Kompetenzentwicklung: Diemersteiner Selbstlerntage und Lerncoaching als intergratives Konzept an der TU Kaiserslautern. Online verfügbar unter: www.uni-kl.de/slzprojekt/dokumente/ upload/792ed_seiten_aus_ herausforderung_kompetenzorientierte_hochschule.pdf (Aufruf am 3.4.2017).

Hessel, S. (2011): Empört euch! Berlin. Online verfügbar unter: www. jerome-segal. de/empoert_euch.pdf (Aufruf am 8.11.2016).

Heyse, V./Erpenbeck, J./Ortmann, S. (Hrsg.) (2015): Kompetenz ist viel mehr. Erfassung und Entwicklung von fachlichen und überfachlichen Kompetenzen in der Praxis. Münster: Waxmann.

Hirschauer, S. (2004): Peer Review Verfahren auf dem Prüfstand. Zum Soziologiedefizit der Wissenschaftsevaluation. In: Zeitschrift für Soziologie, 33, 1, S. 62–83.

Hof, C. (2016): Wissen und Lernen. Versuch einer Systematisierung. In: Hessische Blätter für Volksbildung, 66, 3, S. 205–213.

Holzkamp, K. (1991): Lehren als Lernbehinderung. In: Forum Kritische Psychologie, 27, S. 5–22.

Holzkamp, Klaus. (1993). Lernen: Subjektwissenschaftliche *Grundlegung*. Stuttgart: Klett-Cotta.

Holzkamp, K. (1996): Wider den Lehr-Lern-Kurzschluss. Interview zum Thema ›Lernen‹. In: Arnold, R. (Hrsg.): Lebendiges Lernen. Baltmannsweiler, S. 29–38.

Hüther, G. (2006): Die Macht der inneren Bilder. Wie Visionen das Gehirn, den Menschen und die Welt verändern. 3., durchgesehene Auflage. Göttingen: Vandenhoeck & Ruprecht.

Hüther, G. (2016): Mit Freude lernen—ein Leben lang. Weshalb wir ein neues Verständnis vom Lernen brauchen. Sieben Thesen zu einem erweiterten Lernbegriff und eine Auswahl von Beiträgen zur Untermauerung. Göttingen : Vandenhoeck & Ruprecht.

Ioannidis, J. P. A. (2005): Contradicted and Initially Stronger Effects in Highly Cited Clinical Research. In: *Journal of the American Medical Association*, 294, S. 218–228.

Kaiser, A. (2003): Selbstlernkompetenz. Metakognitive Grundlagen selbstregulierten Lernens und ihre praktische Umsetzung. Köln: ZIEL.

Kaube, J. (2008): Die bibliometrische Verblendung. In: FAZ vom 24. Juli.

Kindl-Beilfuß, C. (2008): Fragen können wie Küsse schmecken. Systemische Fragetechniken für Anfänger und Fortgeschrittene. Heidelberg: Carl-Auer.

Kirchhöfer, D. (2007): Infantilisierung des Lernens? In: Jahrbuch für Pädagogik 2006. Frankfurt a. M. u. a., S. 17–42.

Klafki, W. (1993): Allgemeinbildung heute—Grundzüge internationaler Erziehung. In: Pädagogisches Forum, 1, S. 21–28.

Klemm, H. (2002): Horizont der Erkenntnis. In: Die Zeit vom 3. Januar. Online verfügbar unter: www.zeit.de/2002/02/Horizont_der_Erkenntnis (Aufruf am 20.10.2016).

Kraft, S. (2006): Die Lehre lebt. ›Lehrforschung‹ und Fachdidaktiken für die Weiterbildung. In: Nuissl, E. (Hrsg.): Vom Lehren zum Lernen. Lern- und Lehrforschung für die Weiterbildung. Bielefeld: W. Bertelsmann, S. 209–216.

Kucklick, C. (2015): Die granulare Gesellschaft. Wie das Digitale unsere Wirklichkeit auflöst. 2. Auflage. Berlin: Ullstein.

Kühl, S. (2016): Die vier blinden Flecken der »Theorie U«. In: Wirtschaft und Weiterbildung. Heft 10, S. 24–29.

Kurzweil, R. (2014): Menschheit 2.0. Die Singularität naht. 2., durchgesehene Auflage. Berlin: Lola Books.

Laloux, F. (2015): Reinventing Organizations. Ein Leitfaden zur Gestaltung sinnstiftender Formen der Zusammenarbeit. München: Vahlen.

Lehner, M. (2013): Viel Stoff—wenig Zeit. Wege aus der Vollständigkeitsfalle. 4. Auflage. Bern: Haupt.

Lenzen, D. (1997): Lösen die Begriffe Selbstorganisation, Autopoiesis und Emergenz den Bildungsbegriff ab? Niklas Luhmann zum 70. Geburtstag. In: Zeitschrift für Pädagogik, 43, 6, S. 949–968.

Liessmann, K. P. (2016): Geisterstunde. Die Praxis der Unbildung. Eine Streitschrift. München: Paul Zsolnay.

Livingston, D. W. (2006): Informal Learning: Conceptual Distinction and Preliminary Findings. In: Bekerman, Z./Burbules, N. C./Silberman-Keller, D. (Hrsg.): *Learning Places. The Informal Education Reader.* New York: Peter Lang Publishing Inc., S. 65–91.

Löffler, U. (2001): Die Ausbildungen dauern heute viel zu lange. Halbwertszeit von Wissen beträgt im Internet ein Jahr. In: Deutscher Bildungsserver, Innovationsportal. Das Online-Magazin zum Thema Innovation und Qualitätsentwicklung im Bildungswesen vom 15. März. Online verfügbar unter: http://www.bildungsserver.de/innovationsportal/bildungplus.html?artid=40&mstn=1 (Aufruf am 3.4.2017).

Luhmann, N. (2005): Die Autopoiesis des Bewusstseins. In: Ders.: Soziologische Aufklärung 6. Die Soziologie und der Mensch. 2. Auflage. Wiesbaden: Springer, S. 55–198.

Marinić, J. (2016): Radikal hoffen. In: Süddeutsche Zeitung vom 19./20. November, S. 6. Online verfügbar unter: http://www.sueddeutsche.de/politik/kolumne-radikal-hoffen-1.3255987 (Aufruf am 3.4.2017).

Maturana, H./Varela, F. J. (1987): Der Baum der Erkenntnis: Wie wir die Wirklichkeit durch unsere Wahrnehmung erschaffen—die biologischen Wurzeln des menschlichen Erkennens. 3. Auflage. Bern: Goldmann.

Maturana, H./Yañes, X. D./Muñoz, S. R. (2017): Ethical Reflections—Robots, Living Systems and Human Beings. In: Arnold/Neuser (Hrsg.): Die Beobachtung des Wissens—Das Wissen des Beobachters. Annäherung an eine systemische Hermeneutik. Baltmannsweiler: Schneider Hohengehren, S. 93–106.

Meyer, B./Haywood, N./Sachdev, D./Faraday, S. (2008): What Is Independent Learning and What Are the Benefits for Students? London. In: www.curee.co.uk/files/publication/(site-timestamp)/Whatisindependentlearningandwhatarethebenefits.pdf (Aufruf am 10.11.2016).

Mitscherlich, A. (1996): Auf dem Weg zur vaterlosen Gesellschaft. Ideen zur Sozialpsychologie. 10. Auflage. München: Piper.

Mohle, M./Seidl, D. (2008): Möglichkeiten der Steuerung des Beraters durch den Klienten. In: Bamberger, I. (Hrsg.): Strategische Unternehmensberatung. Konzeptionen—Prozesse—Methoden. 5. Auflage. Wiesbaden: Gabler, S. 249–272.

Müller, A. (1999): Nachhaltiges Lernen. Oder: Was die Schule mit Abnehmen zu tun hat. Beatenberg: Hep.

Murphy, S./Smith, M. A. (1992): Writing Portfolios. A Bridge from Teaching to Assessment. Markham/Ontario: Pippin.

Neuser, W. (2013): Wissen begreifen. Zur Selbstorganisation von Erfahrung, Handlung und Begriff. Wiesbaden: Springer.

Neuser, W. (2017): Der menschliche Beobachter in der Wissensgesellschaft. In: Arnold, R./Neuser, S. Beobachtung des Wissens—Das Wissen des Beobachters: Annäherung an eine systemische Hermeneutik. Baltmannsweiler: Schneider, S. 67–82.

Nietzsche, F. (1972): Nietzsches Werke. Kritische Gesamtausgabe. Bd. VIII3: Nachgelasssene Fragmente Anfang 1888–Anfang Januar 1889. Hrsg. von G. Colli und M. Montinari. Berlin u.a: De Gruyter.

Nowotny, H./Scott, P./Gibbson, M. (2001): Re-thinking Science, Knowledge and the Public in an Age of Uncertainty. Oxford: Polity.

Nüse, R. (1995): Über die Erfindungen des Radikalen Konstruktivismus. 2. Auflage. Weinheim: Deutscher Studienverlag.

Peters, D. P./Ceci, S. J. (1982): Peer Review Practices of Psychological Journals: The Fate of Published Articles, Submitted Again. In: Behavioral and Brain Science, 5, S. 187–195.

Piaget, J. (1981): Jean Piaget über Jean Piaget. Sein Werk aus seiner Sicht. München: Kindler.

Pongratz, L. A. (2010): Sammlung. Fundstücke aus 30 Hochschuljahren. Darmstadt: tuprints.

Pongratz, L. A. (2014): Widersinnig, unnötig, unkritisch: Die konstruktivistische Wende in der Pädagogik. In: www.bildung-wissen.eu/fachbeitraege/widersinnig-unnoetig-unkritisch-die-konstruktivistische-wende-in-der-paedagogik.html (Veröffentlicht am 11.11.14).

Popper, K. (1957): Die offene Gesellschaft und ihre Feinde. Bd. II. Bern: Francke.

Popper, K. (1974): Logik der Sozialwissenschaften. In: Adorno, T. W./Dahrendorf, R./Habermas, J./Popper, K. R.: Der Positivismusstreit in der deutschen Soziologie. Darmstadt/Neuwied: Luchterhand, S. 103–123.

Pörksen, B. (2008): Die Gewissheit der Ungewissheit. Gespräche zum Konstruktivismus. Zweite Auflage. Heidelberg: Carl-Auer-Systeme.

pte pte (2007): Wikipedia lässt Brockhaus alt aussehen. Online verfügbar unter: http://www.computerwoche.de/a/wikipedia-laesst-brockhaus-alt-aussehen,1849919 (Aufruf am 28.4.2017).

Reich, K. (2002): Konstruktivismus—Eine Einführung in das konstruktivistische Denken unter Aufnahme von 10 häufig gehörten kritischen Einwänden. In: Fragner, J./Greiner, U./Vorauer, M. (Hrsg.): Menschenbilder. Zur Auslöschung der anthropologischen Differenz. Schriften der Pädagogischen Akademie des Bundes in Oberösterreich. Bd. 15. Linz: Trauner, S. 91–112.

Ricken, N./Schimank, U. (2012): Wie viel Wissen brauchen wir? Und welches Wissen brauchen wir? Verständigungen über Bildung zwischen Wissenschaft, Wirtschaft und Politik. In: Wolfgang-Ritter-Stiftung (Hrsg.): Wie viel Wissen brauchen wir? Und welches Wissen brauchen wir? Verständigungen über Bildung zwischen Wissenschaft, Wirtschaft und Politik. 24. Universitäts-Gespräche am 10. Und 11. November 2011. Oldenburg, S. 9–16.

Robinsohn, S. B. (1970): Bildungsreform als Revision des Curriculum. Neuwied: Luchterhand.

Rohs, M. (Hrsg.) (2016): Handbuch Informelles Lernen. Wiesbaden.

Rolff, H.-G. (2007): Studien zu einer Theorie der Schulentwicklung. Weinheim u. Basel: Beltz.

Roll, E. (2016): Die Lüge. Was bedeutet es für die Politik, wenn Fakten nicht mehr zählen? In: Süddeutsche Zeitung Nr. 268., vom 19./20. November, S. 49.

Rosa, H./Endres, W. (2016): Resonanzpädagogik. Wenn es im Klassenzimmer knistert. Weinheim: Beltz.

Roth, G. (2007): Persönlichkeit, Entscheidung und Verhalten. Warum es so schwierig ist, sich und andere zu verändern. Stuttgart: Klett-Cotta.

Roth, G./Lück, M. (2010): Mit Gefühl und Motivation lernen. Neurobiologische Grundlagen der Wissensvermittlung im Training. In: Weiterbildung. Zeitschrift für Grundlagen, Praxis und Trends. Heft 1, S. 40–43.

Schiefner-Rohs, M. (2015): Lehrerbildung und digitale Medien. Herausforderungen entlang der Lehrerbildungskette. In: Diess./Gómez Tutor, C./Menzer, C. (Hrsg.): Lehrer.Bildung.Medien. Herausforderungen für die Entwicklung und Gestaltung von Schule. Baltmannsweiler: Schneider Hohengehren, S. 119–128.

Schmidt, S.J. (1998): Die Zähmung des Blicks. Konstruktivismus—Empirie—Wissenschaft. Frankfurt a. M: Suhrkamp.

Schmitz, E. (1984): Erwachsenenbildung als lebensweltbezogener Erkenntnisprozess. In: Enzyklopädie Erziehungswissenschaft. Bd. 11. Stuttgart, S. 95–123.

Schneider, J. R. (2016): Herkunft, Schicksal und Freiheit. Das Gruppenunbewusste in Familiensystemen und Familienaufstellungen. Heidelberg: Carl-Auer.

Schüppel, J. (1996): Wissensmanagement. Organisatorisches Lernen im Spannungsfeld von Wissens und Lernbarrieren. Wiesbaden: Deutscher Universitätsverlag (Gabler-Edition Wissenschaft).

Senge, P. (1996): Die fünfte Disziplin. Stuttgart: Schäffer-Poeschel.

Senge, P./Smith, B./Kruschwitz, N./Laur, J./Schley, S. (2011): Die notwendige Revolution. Wie Individuen und Organisationen zusammenarbeiten, um eine nachhaltige Welt zu schaffen. Heidelberg: Carl-Auer.

Sennett, R. (1998): Der flexible Mensch. Die Kultur des neuen Kapitalismus. Berlin: Berlin Verlag.

Sesink, W. (2006): Bildungstheorie. Skript zur Vorlesung TUD SS 2006. Online verfügbar unter: http://www.abpaed.tu-darmstadt.de/media/arbeitsbereich_bildung_und_technik/gesammelteskripte/ bth_2006_kompl.pdf (Aufruf am 03.05.2017).

Siebert, H. (2011): Selbsteinschließende Reflexion als pädagogische Kompetenz. In: Arnold, R. (Hrsg.): Veränderung durch Selbstveränderung. Impulse für das Changemanagement. Baltmannsweiler: Schneider Hohengehren, S. 9–18.

Siebert, H. (2015): Erwachsene—lernfähig aber unbelehrbar. Was der Konstruktivismus für die politische Bildung leistet. Schwalbach/Ts: Wochenschau.

Simon, F. B. (1999): Die Kunst, nicht zu lernen und andere Paradoxien in Psychotherapie, Management und Politik. 2. Auflage. Heidelberg: Carl-Auer.

Simon, F. B. (2006): Einführung in Systemtheorie und Konstruktivismus. Heidelberg: Carl-Auer.

Spaemann, R. (1994/1995): Wer ist ein gebildeter Mensch? In: Scheideweg. Jahresschrift für skeptisches Denken, 24, S. 34–37.

Spitzer, M. (2007): Lernen. Gehirnforschung und die Schule des Lebens. München: Spektrum Akademischer.

Spurr, S. (2016): Künstliche Intelligenz und Automatisierung: Die Pädagogik ist herausgefordert. Ausblicke aus schulischer Perspektive. In: Vodafone Stiftung, S.36–56.

Steinbach, G. (2016): Arbeiten mit Geschichten. 50 Geschichten mit Gesprächsleitfaden und praktischen Ideen. Augsburg: ZIEL.

Strenger, C. (2015): Zivilisierte Verachtung: Eine Anleitung zur Verteidigung unserer Freiheit. Frankfurt a. M: Suhrkamp.

Stroh, C. (2016): Die Outcomeorientierung als Herausforderung für deutsche Hochschulen. Entwicklung eines Kompetenzmodells für einen Bachelorstudiengang »Integrative Sozialwissenschaften« auf Grundlage des Deutschen Qualifikationsrahmens. Baltmannsweiler: Schneider Hohengehren.

Tietgens, H. (1986): Erwachsenenbildung als Suchbewegung. Annäherungen an eine Wissenschaft von der Erwachsenenbildung Klinkhardt: Bad Heilbrunn/OBB.

Türcke, C. (2016): Lehrerdämmerung. Was die neue Lernkultur in den Schulen anrichtet. München: C.H.Beck.

Ulrich, B. (2016): . . . und doch nicht am Ende. Ein gefährlicher Mann zieht ins Weiße Haus ein. Warum Europa jetzt die westliche Welt verteidigen muss—und das auch kann. In: Die Zeit vom 10. November, S. 3.

Varela, F./Thompson, E./Rosch, E. (1992): Der Mittlere Weg der Erkenntnis. Der Brückenschlag zwischen wissenschaftlicher Theorie und menschlicher Erfahrung. Bern u. a: Scherz.

Vereinigung der Bayerischen Wirtschaft, VbW (Hrsg.) (2003): Bildung neu denken! Das Zukunftsprojekt. Opladen: Springer.

Vereinigung der Bayerischen Wirtschaft, vbw (Hrsg.) (2015): Bildung. Mehr als Fachlichkeit. Gutachten. Münster: Waxmann.

Vodafone Stiftung Deutschland (Hrsg.) (2016): Algorithmen und Aristoteles. Auf der Suche nach der richtigen Bildung für das digitale Zeitalter. Berlin: Tempus Corporate.

Vollmer, G. (1988): Evolutionäre Erkenntnistheorie. Stuttgart: Hirzel S.

Vollmer, G. (1991): Ordnung durch Chaos. Zur Weltbildfunktion wissenschaftlicher Erkenntnis. In: Universitas, 8, S. 761–773.

von Glasersfeld, E. (1996): Radikaler Konstruktivismus. Ideen, Ergebnisse, Probleme. Frankfurt a. M: Suhrkamp.

Walter, U. (2013): Mythos »Halbwertzeit des Wissens«. In: https://www.welt.de/wissenschaft/article160307961/Mythos-Halbwertszeit-des-Wissens.html (Aufruf am 7.8.2013).

Wanken, S. (2016): Außergewöhnliche Weiterbildungskarrieren. Interpretationen von Lernbegründungen Qualifizierter beim Übergang zur wissenschaftlichen Weiterbildung. Norderstedt.

Watzlawick, P. (1988): Anleitung zum Unglücklichsein. München.

Weichert, S. (2016): Wie wird die digitale Hochschule aussehen? In: www. zeit. de/2016/07/digitalisierung-hochschule-studium-internet-vorlesungen (Aufruf am 22.10.2016).

Wolff, C. (2008): Die Halbwertzeit der Wissenszwerge. Anmerkungen zu einigen Mythen der Wissensgesellschaft. In: Geisenhanslücke, A./ Rott, H. (Hrsg.): Ignoranz: Nichtwissen, Vergessen und Mißverstehen in Prozessen kultureller Transformationen. Bielefeld: transcript, S.7–32.

Zajonc, A. (2014): Contemplative Pedagogy in Higher Education. Toward a More Reflective Academy. In: Gunnlaugson, u. a. (Hrsg.) (2014): Contemplative Learning and Inquiry across Disciplines. New York: SUNY Press, S. 1–29.

Zankl, H. (2003): Fälscher, Schwindler, Scharlatane: Betrug in Forschung und Wissenschaft. Weinheim: Wiley-VCH.

Zankl, H. (2004): Der große Irrtum. Wo die Wissenschaft sich täuschte. Darmstadt: Primus.

# About the author

**Rolf Arnold**, PhD, obtained his doctorate at the University of Heidelberg, Germany, in 1983 and his postdoctoral qualification at the Distance University of Hagen, Germany, in 1987. Since 1990, he has been professor of pedagogy (vocational and adult education) at Technische Universität Kaiserslautern, Germany. He is also scientific director of the Distance and Independent Studies Centre (DISC), Kaiserslautern, Germany, and speaker of the Virtual Campus Rhineland-Palatinate (VCRP).